DICKENS ON THE ROMANTIC SIDE
OF FAMILIAR THINGS

ON THE ROMANTIC SIDE
OF FAMILIAR THINGS:

BLEAK HOUSE

and the Novel Tradition

by
ROBERT NEWSOM

1977
COLUMBIA UNIVERSITY PRESS
New York

The Andrew W. Mellon Foundation,
through a special grant, has
assisted the Press in publishing
this volume.

Library of Congress Cataloging in Publication Data

Newsom, Robert, 1944–
    Dickens on the romantic side of familiar things.

    Bibliography: p.
    Includes index.
    1. Dickens, Charles, 1812–1870.   Bleak house.
I. Title.
PR4556.N45   823'.8   77-23476
ISBN 0-231-04244-2

Columbia University Press
New York   Guildford, Surrey

To Linda

PREFACE

NO informed study of Dickens would be possible without the enormous labors of previous Dickensians. This book has benefited incalculably from their work, and my debt to them is very great and should be recorded at the very outset.

I have tried to footnote fully sources for all factual material. It has proven considerably more difficult—and considerably less practicable—to alert the reader to all the critical observations in the large body of literature on Dickens and *Bleak House* that have aided my work. Great masterpieces like *Bleak House* have a happy way of inspiring the critics who write about them, and there is very little that has been written about the novel that I have not found helpful in one way or another. To cite every article that has added something to my reading of it would have produced a quite monstrous apparatus, and to cite every third or fourth article would have been arbitrary and misleading. I have therefore restricted references to critical sources to those whose influence on me has been direct and immediate, and I have largely excluded references to sources that have proven obliquely relevant or suggestive.

I first worked out the lines of my argument in 1970–72. Since then, the Dickens industry has produced a number of important new studies. These have not been incorporated into the footnotes, with a few important exceptions. Chief among these

PREFACE

is Fred Kaplan's *Dickens and Mesmerism: The Hidden Springs of Fiction* (Princeton: Princeton University Press, 1975), a work that very ably documents and discusses Dickens's interest in a phenomenon that I believe is crucial to his art. It is, in any event, central to the argument of this book.

When this study was at an early stage, many friends and colleagues endured long hours of discussion about *Bleak House* with me and read portions of manuscript. Their interest and loyalty have helped me to keep my critical footing in the midst of this endlessly slippery novel. I want to thank particularly Robert L. Caserio, Jr., Myron Magnet, Bernard Rose, and Florian Stuber. I am grateful also to Carl Woodring for his always apt editorial guidance and for sharing both his inexhaustible common sense and equally inexhaustible knowledge of the nineteenth century with me, and to Arnold M. Cooper, Michael Riffaterre, and Michael Rosenthal for their useful comments on an earlier version of portions of this study.

Work done in England was made possible by a grant from The Columbia University Council for Research in the Humanities, which provided me with the happy opportunity of thanking further Graham Storey (editor, with Madeline House and Kathleen Tillotson, of The Pilgrim Edition of the letters), who most graciously opened his files of as yet unpublished Dickens letters to me, and John Greaves, Michael Slater, and Marjorie Pillers, who most graciously opened the innumerable resources, material and spiritual, of the Dickens House to me.

My greatest debts are to Lionel Trilling, who with great kindness and thoughtfulness read early and late versions of my manuscript, to Steven Marcus, who has guided me and encouraged me at every stage of this work, and who may further

PREFACE

be said to have gotten the whole thing underway in the days when I was an undergraduate at Columbia College by reintroducing me to Dickens after first having taught me how to read, and above all to my dear wife, Linda Georgianna, whose keen interest and high enthusiasm, at a time when the world of the university has sometimes seemed to me as bleak and capricious even as the world of Chancery, have more than anything else encouraged me to bring this book to completion.

Costa Mesa, California   ROBERT NEWSOM
June 1977

CONTENTS

A NOTE ON REFERENCES
AND EDITIONS

The text of Dickens's works I have used is that of the Charles
Dickens Edition as reprinted in the Gadshill Edition (London,
1897–99). References, Arabic numerals enclosed in parenthe-
ses, are to chapters.

I have also made use of the following abbreviations for works
often cited:

BH: *Bleak House.*
RP: *Reprinted Pieces.*
HW: *Household Words.*
AYR: *All the Year Round.*
MP: *Miscellaneous Papers*, ed. B. W. Matz in The Na-
           tional Edition (London: Chapman and Hall, 1908).
Forster: John Forster, *The Life of Charles Dickens* (London,
           1872–74 and subsequently revised). The best edition
           is J. W. T. Ley's (London: Palmer, 1928), but as
           this is now very scarce I have given references sim-
           ply to book and chapter.
Johnson: Edgar Johnson, *Charles Dickens: His Tragedy and
           Triumph* (Boston: Little, Brown, 1952).
Nonesuch
Letters: *The Letters of Charles Dickens*, ed. Walter Dexter
           (London: Nonesuch, 1938).

REFERENCES AND EDITIONS

MDGH
Letters: *The Letters of Charles Dickens: Edited by his Sister-in-Law and his Eldest Daughter*, ed. Georgina Hogarth and Mamie Dickens (London, 1880–82), revised and enlarged, with letters to Wilkie Collins, in The National Edition, ed. B. W. Matz (London: Chapman and Hall, 1908).

Coutts
Letters: *The Heart of Charles Dickens*, ed. Edgar Johnson (New York: Duell, Sloan and Pearce, 1952).

It should be noted that the standard texts of Dickens's works (The Charles Dickens Edition) and of his letters (Nonesuch Letters) are being superseded by The Clarendon Dickens (Oxford: Clarendon, in progress) and The Pilgrim Edition of *The Letters of Charles Dickens* (Oxford: Clarendon, in progress). Three novels (*Oliver Twist*, *The Mystery of Edwin Drood*, and *Dombey and Son*), a volume each of Speeches and Readings, and three volumes of a projected twelve of letters (1820–39, 1840–41, and 1842–43) have at this writing been published. I have not had occasion to quote from any of these, nor from George Ford and Sylvère Monod's edition of *Hard Times* for the Norton Critical Editions, which supersedes that of The Charles Dickens Edition. Regrettably, the same editors' edition of *Bleak House* (for the same series) had not appeared at the time this book went to press.

DICKENS ON THE ROMANTIC SIDE
OF FAMILIAR THINGS

CHAPTER ONE

INTRODUCTORY

In Bleak House, I have purposely dwelt upon
the romantic side of familiar things.
—Preface to *Bleak House*

AT the very beginning of Dickens's career, one of the
first of his reviewers described the special effect achieved
by this new and generally unknown young writer as "the romance, as it were, of real life." [1] Since then, almost every
Dickens critic has reached for the same thought. G. K. Chesterton characteristically heightens the paradox: "Dickens used reality," he writes, "while aiming at an effect of romance." [2] But
most often we read—and it is not quite the same thing—of
Dickens's simply mixing or fusing the marvelous and the commonplace. Thus Edgar Johnson tells us, "No writer so inti-
mately fuses the familiar and the strange as Dickens does" and
Philip Collins presents the works as "a mixture of fact and
fancy, of accurate specific local and temporal fact and of highly,
indeed, ostentatiously, fictional contrivances." [3]

Dickens himself would have been perfectly at home with
these judgments, for they closely parallel the remark he casually

INTRODUCTORY

drops, almost as an afterthought, at the end of his preface: "In
Bleak House I have purposely dwelt upon the romantic side of
familiar things."

This book is an extended gloss on that phrase, "the romantic side of familiar things," which has often been cited but sel-
dom discussed.[4] Its thesis is that, properly understood, the
phrase describes with extraordinary precision the central imaginative principle of Dickens's art, a principle that operates with
greatest purity and intensity in *Bleak House*, but which further
can be seen as an essential *novelistic* principle. My final aim has
thus been to bring Dickens back into the center of the tradition
of the English novel and of English literature, rather than leave
him, as is so often the case among both defenders and detrac-
tors, on the outside of the tradition as an unassimilable popular
giant.

One reason that the phrase "the romantic side of familiar
things" has not attracted more discussion is, perhaps, that it very
clearly draws upon Dickens's well-known notions of what art
and literature of all sorts should teach its audience. The phrase
specifically recalls the language of Dickens's announcement of
policy on the first page of the first number of *Household Words*,
written only a year and a half before the writing of *Bleak House*
was begun:

> No mere utilitarian spirit, no iron binding of the mind to
> grim realities, will give a harsh tone to our *Household Words*. In
> the bosoms of the young and old, of the well-to-do and of the
> poor, we would tenderly cherish that light of Fancy which is in-
> herent in the human breast; which, according to its nurture,
> burns with an inspiring flame, or sinks into a sullen glare, but
> which (or woe betide that day!) can never be extinguished. To

2

show to all, that in all familiar things, even in those which are repellent on the surface, there is Romance enough, if we will find it out:—to teach the hardest workers at this whirling wheel of toil, that their lot is not necessarily a moody, brutal fact, excluded from the sympathies and graces of imagination; to bring the greater and the lesser in degree, together, upon that wide field, and mutually dispose them to a better acquaintance and a kinder understanding—is one main object of our *House-hold Words*.[5]

That this didactic doctrine (which derives, of course, from Dickens's usual master in things didactic, Carlyle) is well exemplified in *Bleak House* has been demonstrated over and over again. That it is the explicit moral of Dickens's next novel, *Hard Times*, needs no demonstration. But if invoking the doctrine explains in a general way what Dickens thought the uplifting effect of dwelling on "the romantic side of familiar things" would be on his audience, it doesn't begin to explain either what the actual effects on an audience are, or, more fundamentally (and rarely examined), what technique the phrase actually signifies.

We can see how little Dickens himself has to tell us about what the phrase "the romantic side of familiar things" might mean by looking at another example of his insistence on the didactic responsibility of writers. (The paragraph I quote is from an unsigned review of Robert Hunt's *The Poetry of Science*, which Dickens contributed to *The Examiner* at the end of 1848.)

The design of Mr. Hunt's volume is striking and good. To show that the facts of science are at least as full of poetry, as the most poetical fancies ever founded on an imperfect observation and a distant suspicion of them (as, for example, among the ancient Greeks); to show that if the Dryades no longer haunt the woods, there is, in every forest, in every tree, in every leaf, and in every ring on every sturdy trunk, a beautiful and wondering creation, always changing, always going on, always bearing testimony to the stupendous workings of Almighty Wisdom, and always leading the student's mind from wonder on to wonder, until he is wrapt and lost in the vast worlds of wonder by which he is surrounded from his cradle to his grave; it is a purpose worthy of the natural philosopher, and salutary to the spirit of the age. To show that Science, truly expounding Nature, can, like Nature herself, restore in some new form whatever she destroys; that, instead of binding us, as some would have it, in stern utilitarian chains, when she has freed us from a harmless superstition, she offers to our contemplation something better and more beautiful, something which, rightly considered, is more elevating to the soul, nobler and more stimulating to the soaring fancy; it is a sound, wise, wholesome object. If more of the learned men who have written on these themes had had it in their minds, they would have done more good, and gathered upon their track many followers on whom its feeblest and most distant trace has only now begun to shine.[6]

Now this is singularly unhelpful—as empty and bad a paragraph as one can find in all of Dickens. It is the sort of paragraph that goes toward justifying Ruskin's famous judgment that Dickens was "a leader of the steam-whistle party *par excellence*." [7] It is even worse than that; it is almost as bad as Mr. Chadband. And most remarkable is how untrue the scheme of things here is to Dickens's experience as it is presented in the novels. This paragraph may describe something like what Dickens wanted to achieve for his readers in *Bleak House*, but, if the history of *Bleak House* criticism is any guide at all, it can scarcely be said to reflect what he has achieved for most readers. There is some wonder in familiar things in *Bleak House*, but there is more of nightmare.

The hypothesis I propose to account for the manifest inability of such statements by Dickens to tell us what "the romantic side of familiar things" means is that Dickens himself is profoundly at odds with himself whenever he touches upon the larger scheme of things in his journalistic and private writings, and that it is only in the novels that he achieves anything like a resolution of his own conflicting views. The phrase, "the romantic side of familiar things," I believe, itself embodies this conflict.

The very beginning of the original preface to *Bleak House* gives us an excellent example of how this is so:

A FEW months ago, on a public occasion, a Chancery judge had the kindness to inform me, as one of a company of some hundred and fifty men and women not laboring under any suspicions of lunacy, that the Court of Chancery, though the shining subject of much popular prejudice (at which point I thought the Judge's eye had a cast in my direction), was almost immaculate. There had been, he admitted, a trivial blemish or so in its rate of progress, but this was exaggerated, and had been entirely owing to the "parsimony of the public;" which guilty public, it appeared, had been until lately bent in the most determined manner on by no means enlarging the number of Chancery judges appointed—I believe by Richard the Second, but any other King will do as well.

This seemed to me too profound a joke to be inserted in the body of this book, or I should have restored it to Conversation Kenge or to Mr. Vholes, with one or other of whom I think it must have originated.

INTRODUCTORY

Here Dickens has generated his own profound joke by setting up a powerful tension between the fictional (romantic) and the real (familiar) worlds; but the joke doesn't quite resolve the tension. The second paragraph says something like this: "Either the judge's remark was too absurd for a work of fiction or too deep for understanding to be included in a work of fiction, otherwise I would, or ought to have restored it to these characters from my novel, either because it is precisely as absurd, and as true to life, as they are, or because such fantastic remarks must have originated in my fantastic creations, which are themselves truer than real life." The point is that it is impossible, without violating Dickens's ambiguous logic, to extract an idea from this paragraph which is not paradoxical; he is not so much saying here that truth is stranger than fiction as that fiction is truer than truth or that truth is falser than fiction. And that claim of course goes far beyond the characteristic argument of Dickens's prefaces, which is that precisely those things people find hardest to believe in his novels are the most literally faithful to real life, whether it be the existence of Jacob's Island or the behavior of Nancy or the possibility of Spontaneous Combustion. It even goes beyond Chesterton's remark that "Dickens used reality while aiming at an effect of romance," for in Chesterton's formulation romance simply subverts an apparent reality while Dickens's continual insistence on the truth of his fiction suggests a profounder tension between the two.

"Things" do not, of course, have "romantic" and "familiar" sides. The qualities "romantic" and "familiar" reside not in things themselves but in our perceptions and imaginings of them. Moreover, the qualities "romantic" and "familiar" are wholly antithetical and, under normal circumstances, mutually exclusive. When something strikes us as romantic, then it ceases to be familiar, and vice versa. But it is just this proposition that Dickens, I believe, typically works against. In *Bleak House*, I hope to show, Dickens has "purposely dwelt upon the romantic side of familiar things," but he has not allowed them to cease to be familiar or to become entirely romantic. Rather, he imposes upon the reader a kind of unsettled and unsettling double perspective which requires us to see things as *at once* "romantic" and "familiar." Obviously, this is not the same thing as the kind of alternating point of view that we are familiar with in many later-nineteenth- and twentieth-century novelists, but something considerably more complex and disturbing. For when objects, events, and even people themselves seem to us at once familiar and strange, then our relationship with those objects, events, and people itself seems to dissolve and our very sense of self (our self being that aspect of ourselves that has relationships) begins to dissolve as well.

Rather than simply merge the "romantic" and the "familiar" into some new synthesis, Dickens sought to keep each quality intensely alive for his audience. That is why to speak of "a *mixture* of fact and fancy" in his work makes some sense, even if it misses the tension that is established in the great novels between those two imaginative poles. We can see Dickens's insistence on the "familiar" as the topical and true to life in the arguments of the prefaces, in the novels themselves, and of course in the journalism. Dickens never lost sight of what he saw as his responsibility to portray accurately what was doing in the world even if by today's journalistic standards most of his reporting was tendentious. But even in the journalism, as we have seen, Fancy was not to be put down. Consider, for another example, the mysterious figure Dickens had once imagined as the chief narrator of *Household Words:*

> I want to suppose a certain SHADOW, which may go into any place, by sunlight, moonlight, starlight, firelight, candlelight, and be in all homes, and all nooks and corners, and be supposed to be cognisant of everything, and go everywhere, without the least difficulty. . . . a kind of semi-omniscient, omnipresent, intangible creature. . . . I want him to loom as a fanciful thing over all London; and to get up a general notion of "What will the Shadow say about this, I wonder? Is the Shadow here?" and so forth.[8]

Here we have a character not merely "romantic," but positively supernatural, and Dickens's delight in his magicality is as intense as his insistence in the reality of the evils he is to expose. But just as facts without fancy entailed for Dickens a deadening of the imagination and "iron binding of the mind to grim realities," so too did the purely supernatural leave him generally unmoved and uninspired. That, at least, is true in the novels. Dickens did occasionally write a ghost story, and generally the occasion was Christmas, for almost all of these are found in the Christmas Books and in the Christmas Numbers of *Household Words* and *All The Year Round.* He pretty plainly disbelieved in ghosts, however, and often scoffed at those who did not. Dickens did indeed believe in some phenomena we tend to regard as supernatural—mesmeric clairvoyance and Spontaneous Combustion, for example. But he also believed that they had been scientifically well-documented.[9] In his public writings he never betrays a weakness for the occult or mystical. In private life he does sometimes turn alternately hard- and soft-headed.

INTRODUCTORY

To a depressed young Danish woman he writes bracingly that "The world is not a dream, but a reality, of which we are the chief part, and in which we must be up and doing something," while he confides to John Forster his quite different sense that "*this* is all a dream, may be, and death will wake us." [10] It is precisely this kind of conflict which informs the phrase "the romantic side of familiar things" and which Dickens tries to resolve in the novels. The point again is that Dickens's fascination is for neither the "romantic" nor the "familiar" singly, but for both together. Or, we could say, his fascination is for the interplay generated by his own profound conflict about them.

We shall see that the force of that tension and the paradoxes engendered by it are a good deal more pronounced than the language usually used to describe it would suggest. But to do that, we shall have to turn to a reading of the novel I have chosen as my test case, *Bleak House*.

CHAPTER TWO

BLEAK HOUSE, I
SUSPENDED ANIMATION

*Everything was so strange—the stranger from
its being night in the day-time, the candles
burning with a white flame, and looking raw and
cold—that I read the words in the newspaper
without knowing what they meant, and found myself
reading the same words repeatedly.*
—*Bleak House*, chapter 3

I

IT is rapidly becoming a commonplace of literary criticism
that while the proper study of mankind may be man, the
proper study of literature is literature—that both the appropriate
subject for and the subject characteristically belonging to literature are its own technique and method. This is the message
brought to us by students of rhetoric, linguistics, and struc-
turalism, and this is the message which has been brought to
bear upon Dickens studies most notably in recent articles by
J. Hillis Miller and Steven Marcus. [1] *"Bleak House,"* Hillis Miller
asserts at the beginning of his Introduction to the Penguin En-

glish Library edition of that novel, "is a document about the interpretation of documents." [2] And while it is true that *any* literary production may be said in a general sense to have its own methods as its subject, it is in a more particular sense true of Dickens's literary productions, and especially true of *Bleak House.*

Miller shows that not only does the novel place the reader in precisely the situation of all those characters who are trying to solve mysteries, but that the writer and the novel as a whole are placed in the perplexed situation of posing what are perhaps *Bleak House*'s most famous questions:

> What connexion can there be, between the place in Lincolnshire, the house in town, the Mercury in powder, and the whereabout of Jo the outlaw with the broom, who had that distant ray of light upon him when he swept the churchyard-step? What connexion can there have been between many people in the innumerable histories of this world, who, from opposite sides of great gulfs, have, nevertheless, been very curiously brought together! (16)

For Miller, the ultimate answer is that there is no answer—at least none that can be articulated, because "The villain is the act of interpretation itself, the naming which assimilates the particular into a system, giving it a definition and a value, incorporating it into a whole." [3] Miller justifies this judgment by pointing on the one hand to the tremendously long list of detectives in the novel whose interpretations are either flatly wrong (like Mrs. Snagsby's) or whose interpretations, while right in themselves, come too late to do any good (like Mr. Bucket's), and on the other hand to the names of characters in the novel, virtually all of which are either "openly metaphorical . . . or seem tantalizingly to contain some covert metaphor lying almost on the surface of the word." [4] "This overt fictionality," Miller continues, "is Dickens's way of demystifying the belief . . . that the right name gives the essence of a thing." On the contrary, "The metaphors in [the characters'] names reveal the fact that they are not real people or even copies of real people. They exist only in language." [5]

Here Miller is going considerably beyond his assertion—which no one I think will disagree with—that "*Bleak House* is a document about the interpretation of documents." To say that characters exist *only* in language demystifies of course a good deal more than the authority of "documents." Curiously, Miller .seems to have put himself in the camp of those critics who come upon Dickens from precisely the opposite direction, those who, insofar as they come to Dickens with the tenets of realism ineradicably in mind (Robert Garis is perhaps the best example here), inevitably find Dickens wanting. Certainly Miller does not want to find Dickens wanting, and it is precisely the tenets of realism that he sets out to demystify. But he overshoots his mark and, brilliantly, demystifies fiction itself.

Bleak House is indeed a document about the interpretation of documents, and of course a large part of the novel is about the falsity of certain kinds of documents; but *Bleak House* itself is presented as an authentic document: nothing in it suggests that we are to question its own authority. There is nothing in Esther's narrative to suggest that she is not telling the truth, and there is nothing in the third-person narrative to suggest that it is not telling the truth. We know *Bleak House* is a novel and that therefore its characters "exist only in language." But what we know is not necessarily the same as what we believe, and I suggest that most readers of the novel believe in its characters. This is even true, I suggest further, of those readers who say things like "there never was such a person as Esther." The very form and ambiguity of such statements attest to the reality of Esther as "a person." And yet Miller is quite right, I believe, to center on the problematic relationship between fiction and reality.

Every reader of the novel quickly recognizes that something peculiar is going on in the way the story is told: the double narrative not only comes upon us without warning in chapter 3, but the very conditions of that narrative are never explained. Esther begins her narrative by telling us that "I have a great deal of difficulty in beginning to write my portion of these pages, for I know I am not clever." But how can Esther know of the existence of the other narrator? The other narrator is an omniscient third-person narrator familiar in the English novel since Fielding. He is one of those characters of whom we may say that he exists "only in language." But by the very rules of his profession, so to speak, his existence cannot be known to Esther, who, as a character in the novel, is a character of an entirely different order. We are not presented, in other words, with a case of multiple narration in which different characters narrate a single story in turn. Nor are we even presented with a first-person narrative supplemented by an omniscient third person narrative, as would be the case if Esther were being helped by an unseen hand. She does see the other hand, and it is that fact that confounds the reader. Rather than being given a shifting point of view, we are given two points of view which are somehow incompatible. Here a fictional reality is not being demystified, but, on the contrary, made doubly problematic.

Of course, it is not only through the double narrative that Dickens makes reality strange. The famous beginning of the novel places us in a world which is both dazzlingly real and dazzlingly unreal:

> LONDON. Michaelmas Term lately over, and the Lord Chancellor sitting in Lincoln's Inn Hall. Implacable November weather. As much mud in the streets, as if the waters had but newly retired from the face of the earth, and it would not be wonderful to meet a Megalosaurus, forty feet long or so, waddling like an elephantine lizard up Holborn Hill. Smoke lowering down from chimney-pots, making a soft black drizzle, with flakes of soot in it as big as full-grown snow-flakes—gone into mourning, one might imagine, for the death of the sun. Dogs, undistinguishable in mire. Horses, scarcely better; splashed to their very blinkers. Foot passengers, jostling one another's umbrellas, in a general infection of ill-temper, and losing their foothold at street-corners, where tens of thousands of other foot passengers have been slipping and sliding since the day broke (if this day ever broke), adding new deposits to the crust upon crust of mud, sticking at those points tenaciously to the pavement, and accumulating at compound interest.

Bleak House begins like a newspaper story, with a dateline. It begins in Lincoln's Inn Hall on the last day or so of November. But it also begins in the early days of the Creation (for "the waters had but newly retired from the face of the earth") or just after the Flood. Or it begins at the end of time (for the flakes of soot have "gone into mourning, one might imagine, for the death of the sun"). Here we have a literal mixing of fact and fancy, and here we can say Dickens is in the most obvious sense dwelling upon "the romantic side of familiar things." But the "romantic" and "familiar" perspectives are not paradoxical or puzzling inasmuch as the perspectives here are quite plainly those of the real eye and the mind's eye.

This opening paragraph is one of the passages Robert Garis has used in defining Dickens's "theatrical mode," and he recalls Gissing's objection that "This darkness visible makes one rather cheerful than otherwise, for we are spectators in the company of a man who allows nothing to balk his enjoyment of life." [6] Gissing's objection becomes Garis's point. "I would amplify Gissing's remark," he tells us, "to say that the source of Dickens's enjoyment here is not only the scene before him, but his own skill in rendering that scene, and that he consciously and proudly offers us that skill for our enjoyment and applause." [7] And presumably this would be Miller's point as well, for the fictionalizing of reality here is entirely overt, as the phrase "one might imagine" makes clear.

If the narrative itself is not puzzling, the scene it narrates surely is. Something *is* wrong in reality, and that something wrong is the fog and mud which render things and people "undistinguishable." Of course we shall almost immediately learn that the fog and mud "stand for" the central evil and confusion, "most pestilent of hoary sinners," the High Court of Chancery. It is because Dickens has chosen as his subject something as bewildered and bewildering as Chancery that the fanciful imaginings of the opening paragraphs are not gratuitous, and not even in that sense fanciful. The "familiar" things here, the fog, the mud, and Chancery—and Chancery was almost as familiar to readers of the newspapers in 1850 as the fog and mud

16

which were a part of their almost daily experience [8]—not only encourage such imaginings, but virtually impose them. That point becomes explicit much later in the novel when Miss Flite says to Esther about Chancery that "there's a dreadful attraction in the place. . . . There's a cruel attraction in the place. You *can't* leave it. And you *must* expect" (35). Miss Flite is of course mad, and her referring to the "spell" of Chancery is her way of signifying that she knows she is mad: she is never so lucid as in this scene with Esther. Chancery has driven her mad as it drives others in the novel mad (most prominently, Tom Jarndyce, Gridley—"mad" in another sense—and, less dramatically, but even more fatally, Richard). But that her madness is an appropriate and even logical response to Chancery is testified to by Esther's comment on first witnessing Chancery proceedings, that "there seemed to be no reality in the whole scene, except poor little Miss Flite, the madwoman, standing on a bench, and nodding at it" (24). Therefore it is *not* especially wonderful that the narrator of the opening pages should fancy himself in a scene at the beginning of time or at the end of time. His own fanciful imagination, we may say, is an important, perhaps essential, part of the reality he is describing.

The "familiar" things in the novel, Dickens is saying, belong to a reality so astonishing that we have to call it unreal, and so astonishing, indeed, that we can no longer experience its components as "familiar." We should be reminded here of the beginning of the novel's preface, which says, among other things, precisely that the reality Dickens is describing is itself too absurd to be represented in a work of fiction. Reality is its own satire.

Thus, even in speaking of *Bleak House*'s opening paragraphs, there is something unsatisfactory about speaking of a mixture of fact and fancy: that formulation misses the problematic quality of Dickens's reality. It misses too Dickens's fascination with the problem; for it is on the problem that his interest clearly centers. More than being concerned to *teach* us how documents which purport to represent reality are misleading and even false, he is, I think, concerned with *dwelling*, to use his own word, on precisely that point in experience when what we have come to think of as the "familiar" suddenly ceases to be so, and strikes us instead as something the very opposite of the "familiar," the "romantic." And the converse, as I hope to show, is true as well: *Bleak House* dwells also on the "familiar" side of "romantic" things.

II

Almost all books that have general arguments may be described as seeking to move the reader from a "familiar" to a "romantic" perception of a thing or from a "romantic" to a "familiar" one. The latter is usually the overt strategy. An author begins with an idea that is new and even bizarre to us—the ideas of natural selection or unconscious motivation, for example. If he has argued well, then at the end of his book his idea will have passed from being something strange and even offensive to being accepted as something we can and must live with. If he has argued with genius, that idea will pass into a commonplace, something we have grown so accustomed to that it becomes an essential part of ourselves. But an author can just as well move us in the opposite direction, from a perception of a thing as "familiar" to a perception of it as "romantic." Malthus, for example, does this in the *First Essay* with the idea of "necessity," an idea straight out of the common language and overlooked for just that reason. By the end of the *First Essay*, the idea of necessity, transparently understood at the outset, has become opaquely understood: it has passed from invisible familiarity to visible strangeness—and frightening reality. Of course, authors of books with such arguments usually move us in both directions at once: Darwin and Freud make old, familiar ideas strange to us while they are familiarizing us with new ones. The notion of free will becomes positively an astonishing conception to us by the time we have read through the first part of the *Introductory Lectures on Psycho-Analysis*.

The point in all of this is that an author with an argument of this kind wants to persuade us of something, which necessarily involves moving us from one position of certainty to quite another position of certainty, and to do this he must take us through some critical peripety. The greater the genius, the more dazzling that peripety is likely to be, and the more likely it is that we as readers will return to that peripety to be dazzled by it again and again. But the peripety is not the point. It really is something we are supposed (by the author) to be carried *through*. In *Bleak House*, we shall see, it really is the point, and it is the point suggested by "the romantic side of familiar things."

We have already seen a few of the ways in which reality is both made strange and is strange in *Bleak House*. But perhaps the best demonstration of how Dickens dwells upon "the romantic side of familiar things" comes from a rather detailed examination of how the whole opening number works, of what questions and expectations, in other words, the first monthly in-

19

stallment raises in its readers. Most importantly, what rules has the opening number set up for the novel's narrative?

One pattern becomes apparent on the novel's first page as the narrator describes the literally chaotic scene before him—literally chaotic because of the war of earthly elements described and perhaps too because this world of *Chancery* suggests a punning connection with not only the "chance people" of the second paragraph but with Chance as one of the traditional rulers of Chaos.[9] The pattern of the opening, and indeed the pattern of things described, is circular. The first four paragraphs of the novel complete a full circle.[10] We begin with "the Lord Chancellor sitting in Lincoln's Inn Hall," move out into the neighboring streets, take in a view of the "Essex marshes" and the "Kentish heights," return again to the London streets and finally to Temple Bar and Lincoln's Inn Hall again. We can only move in circles, moreover, because the world of Chancery is itself circular. It is a world of "interminable briefs" and on this particular afternoon is "mistily engaged in one of the ten thousand stages of an endless cause." Both statements, of course, are wholly self-contradictory—briefs are the opposite of interminable, and a cause that is endless cannot have a finite number of stages—unless those briefs and stages are ranged round a circle. John Jarndyce, in fact, will later speak of "the wheel of Chancery" (35), referring to both the instrument of torture and the wheel of Chance or Fortune. Even the suit in which he is a party, Jarndyce and Jarndyce, is, as its name implies, circular.

> Jarndyce and Jarndyce drones on. This scarecrow of a suit has, in course of time, become so complicated, that no man alive knows what it means. The parties to it understand it least; but it has been observed that no two Chancery lawyers can talk about

it for five minutes, without coming to a total disagreement as to all the premises. Innumerable children have been born into the cause; innumerable young people have married into it; innumerable old people have died out of it. Scores of persons have deliriously found themselves made parties in Jarndyce and Jarndyce, without knowing how or why; whole families have inherited legendary hatreds with the suit. The little plaintiff or defendant, who was promised a new rocking-horse when Jarndyce and Jarndyce should be settled, has grown up, possessed himself of a real horse, and trotted away into the other world. . . . but Jarndyce and Jarndyce still drags its dreary length before the Court, perennially hopeless.

The circular nature of Chancery asserts itself in both the smallest and the largest ways. The "foggy glory" round the Chancellor's head is but the first of an endless series of expanding concentric circles, "and even those who have contemplated its history from the outermost circle of such evil, have been insensibly tempted into a loose way of letting bad things alone to take their own bad course, and a loose belief that if the world go wrong, it was, in some off-hand manner, never meant to go right." No two Chancery lawyers can talk about Jarndyce and Jarndyce "for five minutes without coming to a total disagreement as to all the premises"—they cannot, that is to say, talk about it without immediately becoming deadlocked within one of the smaller circles. And the circles have a life of their own. Jarndyce and Jarndyce was once but a small circle, a mere "scarecrow of a suit," which has grown so large that it now "drags its dreary length before the court, perennially hopeless," rather like that "Megalosaurus, forty feet long or so," whom "it would not be wonderful to meet . . . waddling like an elephantine lizard up Holborn Hill," for like the Megalosaurus it

21

belongs to the distant world out of which we came, and which "no man alive" now understands.

The circle Dickens traces for us in the first four paragraphs is repeated throughout the chapter:

> On such an afternoon, if ever, the Lord Chancellor ought to be sitting here—as here he is—with a foggy glory round his head. . . . This is the Court of Chancery. . . .
> Thus, in the midst of the mud and at the heart of the fog, sits the Lord High Chancellor in his High Court of Chancery.

At first we can understand the world of Chancery no better than those who live in it. We are like those "chance people on the bridges peeping over the parapets," or like "the uninitiated from the streets, who peep in through the glass panes in the door [of Lincoln's Inn Hall]," or like the "little mad old woman" who stands "on a seat at the side of the hall, the better to peer into the curtained sanctuary," or even like the Chancellor himself, "outwardly directing his contemplation to the lantern in the roof, where he can see nothing but fog." We are like them, and they are all like one another, for the fog that at once reveals and conceals the world makes everyone and everything look like everything else. The gas masquerades as the sun, for it looms "through the fog in divers places in the streets, much as the sun may, from the spongy fields, be seen to loom by husbandman and ploughboy." The crowds in the street are anonymous "foot passengers" obscured by mud and fog and their little army of umbrellas, and are "losing their foot-hold at street-corners, where tens of thousands of other foot passengers have been slipping and sliding since the day broke." They are, like every-

one else, mired "in one of the ten thousand stages of an endless
cause." The Chancery practitioners are hardly less anonymous:

> Eighteen of Mr. Tangle's learned friends, each armed with a
> little summary of eighteen hundred sheets, bob up like eighteen
> hammers in a pianoforte, make eighteen bows, and drop into
> their eighteen places of obscurity.

This circular mirroring of people, places, and images with
one another does not let up throughout the whole course of the
novel. Nothing that is introduced in the first pages fails to return either in its own shape or only slightly modified. The
Megalosaurus of the first paragraph returns in the same chapter
as the legendary suit itself, which "drags its dreary length before
the court," but also recurs agains and again in later chapters.
The "wagons and hackney coaches" of the London streets roar
along "like one great dragon" (10). Judy Smallweed "appears to
attain a perfectly geological age, and to date from the remotest
periods" (21); and her grandfather's god, we are told in the same
chapter, is "Compound Interest," which also refers us back to
the novel's first paragraph. "The hot water pipes . . . trail
themselves all over the house" in the "antedeluvian forest" at
Chesney Wold (28), "where old stone lions and grotesque monsters bristled outside dens of shadow, and snarled at the evening
gloom over the escutcheons they held in their grip" (36). Miss
Flite calls Chancery simply "the Monster" (35). The blue bags
containing Chancery documents are "stuffed, out of all regularity of form, as the larger sort of serpents are in their first gorged
state" (39). Mr. Krook's cat, Lady Jane, goes "leaping and
bounding and tearing about . . . like a Dragon" (39). "The

Duke of Poodle sends [to Tulkinghorn's funeral] a splendid pile of dust and ashes, with silver wheel-boxes, patent axles . . . and three bereaved worms, six feet high, holding on behind" (53), while Lady Dedlock is as "indifferent as if all passion, feeling, and interest, had been worn out in the earlier ages of the world, and had perished from its surface with its other departed monsters" (48). And so on.

The Megalosaurus is but the first image in the novel, and we could draw up equally long (or longer) lists for the other images of the first few paragraphs. The "smoke lowering down from Chimney-pots . . . with flakes of soot in it as big as full-grown snow-flakes" recurs at several points, but most dramatically as presaging Krook's death:

> "Why, Tony, what on earth is going on in this house to-night? Is there a chimney on fire?" [asks Mr. Guppy.]
> "Chimney on fire!"
> "Ah!" returns Mr. Guppy. "See how the soot's falling. See here, on my arm! See again, on the table here! Confound the stuff, it won't blow off—smears, like black fat!" (32)

And so too does the confusion between up and down in which the smoke is involved return—in fact in the paragraph following the one I have just quoted:

> They look at one another, and Tony goes listening to the door, and a little way up-stairs, and a little way down-stairs. Comes back, and says it's all right, and all quiet.

In the same chapter, "Mr. Weevle has been down and up, and down and up [from Krook's shop] . . . oftener than before" and, as he converses with Snagsby, glances "up and down the court." Bleak House itself is "one of those delightfully irregular houses where you go up and down steps out of one room into another" (6). Reading an article aloud to the circle at Chesney Wold, Sir Leicester interrupts himself at several points, each time "invariably losing his place after each observation, and going up and down the column to find it again" (29). These repeated up-and-down patterns signify confusion, of course, but also suggest a particularly restless and uneasy variant of the larger pattern of circular repetitions. Allan Woodcourt, "who appears in some inaptitude for sleep to be wandering abroad rather than counting the hours on a restless pillow, strolls, . . . often pauses and looks about him, up and down the miserable by-ways [of Tom-all-Alone's]" (46). The novel's central restless pacer, perhaps, is Lady Morbury Dedlock, the ghost of The Ghost's Walk, who in life had been lamed by a horse and there-after "tried to walk upon the terrace; and with the help of the stone balustrade, went up and down, up and down, up and down, in sun and shadow, with greater difficulty every day" (7).

In his classic exposition of *Bleak House*, Hillis Miller notes that the novel's first chapter creates a world in which everything is in motion, but "it is a motion which does not move any-where." [11] Reading the opening chapter is like watching the workings of a complex machine when all the gears have been disengaged, but continue to turn under their own momentum; indeed, like being caught up in such a machine ourselves. The state we find described and the state in which we find ourselves is therefore literally one of suspended animation, and this be-comes especially clear at the very end of the first chapter. While it describes no real events, the chapter does describe a good deal of activity, and at its end brings us to the brink of a real event. The Chancellor is being waited upon by a boy and girl, wards of Chancery, whom he is about to see in his private room. No sooner is this announced than the chapter closes, and we too are made to wait his decision as to whether they shall live with their uncle or not. The second chapter, "In Fashion," abruptly intervenes, and appears to remove us to an entirely different world. But the difference between being "In Fashion" and "In Chancery" is only apparent. The two worlds explicitly mirror one another: they are "not so unlike," for "both are things of precedent and usage" (2). Both, that is, are devoted to repeating patterns of the past. And the two worlds mirror one another also in what might at first seem small details. The evil of the world of fashion is "that it is a world wrapped up in too much jeweller's cotton and fine wool," which certainly recalls the Chancellor's sitting in Lincoln's Inn Hall, "softly fenced in with crimson cloth and curtains" (1) and the woolsack upon which he sits in the House of Lords and which symbolizes his office.

Again, we are both moving in circles and having them described to us. But the energy with which the circles of the first chapter are turning is here running down, and there is far more suspension than animation in the fashionable world. Lady Dedlock has her "dim little star[s] revolving about her" and is herself turned about the fingers of her tradesmen and servants, as Mr. Sladdery the librarian tells us. But those spits in the kitchen described in the chapter's first paragraph have indeed stopped, and it will be long before they "shall begin to turn prodigiously!"

When we first meet Lady Dedlock she is in the midst of flight:

SUSPENDED ANIMATION

My Lady Dedlock has returned to her house in town for a few days previous to her departure for Paris, where her ladyship intends to stay some weeks; after which her movements are uncertain.

Having been led by our guide out of Chancery and out of London into Lincolnshire, we find ourselves back in London again, at the Dedlock house in town. And at that house

> upon this muddy, murky afternoon, presents himself an old-fashioned old gentleman, attorney-at-law, and eke solicitor of the High Court of Chancery, who has the honour of acting as legal advisor of the Dedlocks, and has as many cast-iron boxes in his office with that name outside, as if the present baronet were the coin of the conjuror's trick, and were constantly being juggled through the whole set. Across the hall, and up the stairs, and along the passages, and through the rooms, which are very brilliant in the season and very dismal out of it—Fairy-land to visit, but a desert to live in—the old gentleman is conducted, by a Mercury in powder, to my Lady's presence.

This is Mr. Tulkinghorn, "surrounded by a mysterious halo of family confidences," like the Chancellor's "foggy glory." His arrival simply completes another circle, for Lady Dedlock is involved in a case in Chancery, and he has come to her this afternoon to advise her what has been doing—though nothing, of course, "has been done."

> Mr. Tulkinghorn takes out his papers, asks permission to place them on a golden talisman of a table at my Lady's elbow, puts on his spectacles, and begins to read by the light of a shaded lamp.
> " 'In Chancery. Between John Jarndyce—' "

My Lady interrupts, requesting him to miss as many of the formal horrors as he can.

Mr. Tulkinghorn glances over his spectacles, and begins again lower down. My Lady carelessly and scornfully abstracts her attention. Sir Leicester in a great chair looks at the fire, and appears to have a stately liking for the legal repetitions and prolixities, as ranging among the national bulwarks. It happens that the fire is hot, where my lady sits; and that the hand-screen is more beautiful than useful, being priceless but small. My Lady, changing her position, sees the papers on the table—looks at them nearer—looks at them nearer still—asks impulsively:

"Who copied that?"

Mr. Tulkinghorn stops short, surprised by my Lady's animation and her unusual tone.

"Is it what you people call law-hand?" she asks, looking full at him in her careless way again, and toying with her screen.

"Not quite. Probably"—Mr. Tulkinghorn examines it as he speaks—"the legal character which it has, was acquired after the original hand was formed. Why do you ask?"

"Anything to vary this detestable monotony. O, go on, do!"

Mr. Tulkinghorn reads again. The heat is greater, my Lady screens her face. Sir Leicester dozes, starts up suddenly, and cries, "Eh? what do you say?"

"I say I am afraid," says Mr. Tulkinghorn, who had risen hastily, "that Lady Dedlock is ill."

"Faint," my Lady murmurs, with white lips, "only that; but it is like the faintness of death. Don't speak to me. Ring, and take me to my room."

The completion of this circle takes us back to the very beginning, to the title of the first chapter. And no sooner is this circle completed than the novel finally appears to get under way, after some dozen or so pages, and presents us with its first real event. It is the event, moreover, which springs the action of the whole novel, for it is Lady Dedlock's "imprudence" here, her being "taken by surprise" (40), that sets Tulkinghorn off on the investigation that will finally expose her and lead to his own death. Only the merest *chance* sets things in motion. It "happens" that the fire is too warm and that Lady Dedlock's hand-screen—the symbolism is obvious—"is more beautiful than useful." "Changing her position," her attention, which she had "carelessly and scornfully" abstracted, is now drawn to the paper Mr. Tulkinghorn is reading, and recognizing the hand as Captain Hawdon's she lets down her guard for an instant and "asks impulsively" her fateful question. But no sooner has the question been asked and the action begun than it comes to a stop again. "Mr. Tulkinghorn stops short, surprised by my Lady's animation and her unusual tone." Immediately we are back again in the "detestable monotony" of the suspended animation of the fashionable world. Mr. Tulkinghorn takes up his reading again, and Sir Leicester, though he "appears to have a stately liking for the legal repetitions and prolixities," has fallen into a doze and back into the world of Rip Van Winkles and sleeping beauties invoked at the beginning of the chapter. Lady Dedlock grows ill and faint, and Sir Leicester is awakened and "starts up suddenly," but he wakes in a world that is itself still largely asleep. The "stopped spits in the kitchen" have not yet begun "to turn prodigiously," and Sir Leicester can explain away his Lady's faintness by remarking that "the weather is extremely trying—and she really has been bored to death down at our place in Lincolnshire."

As we have seen, *Bleak House* is not a novel that gets under way easily. The opening chapter leaves us on the brink of an event, is interrupted by another chapter which finally does present us with an event, only to lapse again into sleepy obscurity. It is not surprising that the third chapter, introducing Esther's narrative, should repeat the pattern:

> I have a great deal of difficulty in beginning to write my portion of these pages, for I know I am not clever. I always knew that. I can remember, when I was a very little girl indeed, I used to say to my doll, when we were alone together, "Now Dolly, I am not clever, you know very well, and you must be patient with me, like a dear!" And so she used to sit propped up in a great arm-chair, with her beautiful complexion and rosy lips, staring at me—or not so much at me, I think, as at nothing—while I busily stitched away, and told her every one of my secrets.

Like the Chancellor, who has his "satellites" (8) and Lady Dedlock, who has her "dim little star[s] revolving about her" (2), Esther is at the center of a circle and is the center of her world. Her name means "a star" [12] and there is of course a pun intended in her surname: she is the summer sun. But her world does not at first seem very much to resemble that of the Chancellor or of Lady Dedlock. It is removed from theirs in place and time. Windsor lies outside the apparent orbit we have described around Chancery, Chesney Wold, and the Dedlock house in town, and we have evidently left the "muddy, murky afternoon" on which the novel began. Esther's doll does recall—and comment upon—the Chancellor and Lady Dedlock, for she sits "propped up in a great arm-chair, with her beautiful complexion and rosy lips, staring at . . . nothing." And like Mr. Tulkinghorn she is the (literally) "silent depository" (2) of family secrets. Esther too is a silent observer. "I had always a rather noticing way," she says, "a silent way of noticing what passed before me." Nevertheless, what seems to be missing from her world are the mud and the fog of the first chapter, and the kind of animation-in-suspension which they create. The story of her early life, which begins her narrative, appears to be a succession of orderly and intelligible events. But Esther gets no more than a couple of pages into her story before our way again becomes obscure.

> It was my birthday. There were holidays at school on other birthdays—none on mine. There were rejoicings at home on other birthdays, as I knew from what I had heard the other girls relate to one another—there were none on mine. My birthday was the most melancholy day at home, in the whole year.
>
> I have mentioned, that, unless my vanity should deceive me (as I know it may, for I may be very vain, without suspecting it—though indeed I don't), my comprehension is quickened when my affection is. My disposition is very affectionate; and perhaps I might still feel such a wound, if such a wound could be received more than once, with the quickness of that birthday.

The meaning of this important passage is generally clear: Esther is about to relate the story of an especially awful birthday, one which, because of her unusual sensitivity, has been so deeply wounding that the pain of it can be recalled only partially. It is the kind of passage, further, that is not especially liable to stop us on a first reading (like our first view of Lady Dedlock) for we are eager to know just what that wound might be. If we do pause, however, we see that the second paragraph here in fact does not really make sense. The trouble begins in the parenthetical clause, "I may be very vain, without suspecting it—though indeed I don't." "Don't" what? "Don't" *not* suspect it, which is what the syntax seems to demand, but the sense would make nonsensical? The problem is not simply grammatical, but logical. Esther is caught up in a vicious circle: she may be vain, without suspecting it, but she clearly *does* suspect it, so her first statement cannot be true. The rest of the paragraph poses even greater logical problems:

> . . . my comprehension is quickened when my affection is. My disposition is very affectionate; and perhaps I might still feel such a wound, if such a wound could be received more than once, with the quickness of that birthday.

The implicit conclusion to the first few clauses is clear. If her understanding is greater when her sympathies are engaged, and if they are usually engaged (as her having a "very affectionate" disposition would imply), then she is usually quick to comprehend—a complete contradiction of her earlier statement that she "had always a rather noticing way—not a quick way, O no!" Esther is caught again in the same confusion I have just discussed. On the one hand she suspects and understands, and on the other something prevents her either from suspecting or understanding, or from admitting that she both suspects and understands. This confusion—so typical of Esther, and so annoying to many of her critics—manifests itself in various ways in the paragraph. There is no logical connection between the first two clauses of the last sentence. What do comprehension or an affectionate disposition have to do with still feeling "such a wound"? The "wound" appears out of nowhere, for it refers not to anything she has already mentioned but to the recollections she is about to relate. And the last two clauses are entirely ambiguous. Does she mean that she might still feel such a wound if it could be felt again with the quickness with which she first felt it, or that it is the nature of such wounds to be felt with such quickness only once? Does "quickness," in other words, refer to feeling or to receiving the wound? What, finally, is the connection between comprehension, feeling, and receiving, which seem to be equated here but which are not at all the same things?

Esther seems to be talking more to herself than to her audience here. The tone is musing and abstracted, and that would both account for the incoherence of her thoughts and provide us with another way of understanding them. For it is characteristic of such states that they present us with what are apparently quasi-logical connections in syntax which only serve to obscure the real train of our thought.[13] We have seen that the connections here simply don't work, and that the logic of Esther's thoughts is only apparent. Indeed, we can perhaps dispense with them as artifacts. What this leaves us with is the following series of words: "comprehension . . . quickened . . . affection . . . disposition . . . affectionate . . . wound . . . quickness." This series might not at first seem meaningful, but it does in fact have its own inner coherence. "Comprehension" and "quickness" are obviously related: a "quick" person being one who is unusually perceptive. But "quickness" is also related to "affection." Being "quickened" can mean the same thing as being "affected"; that is, being deeply stirred. "Affection" in turn can mean any emotional "disposition" and also, in its medical sense, something like a "wound." Similarly, a "wound" can mean the raw flesh of the "quick," and "quickness" takes us back again to "comprehension."

Esther's thought proceeds not by logical steps but by a series of words with overlapping meanings, and a series, moreover, which is circular. It is in the very texture of her thoughts, in other words, that we are presented with the same kind of stop-and-go, circular motion that seems to be the external condition of things in the worlds of Chancery and of fashion. The mud and fog of the first two chapters, signifying confusions in the external relations between things and people, have in the third been internalized and become the inhibited condition of a particular kind of thinking. Chancery thus represents both society and a state of mind—specifically Esther's state of mind, and the state of mind, therefore, of a large part of the novel itself.

One of the other most important circular reverberations of Esther's first chapter with the worlds of Chancery and fashion comes when Esther relates the stories of her melancholy birthday and of her godmother's death:

. . . my godmother and I were sitting at the table before the fire. . . . I happened to look timidly up from my stitching, across the table, at my godmother, and I saw in her face, looking gloomily at me, "It would have been far better, little Esther, that you had had no birthday; that you had never been born!"

I broke out crying and sobbing, and I said, "O, dear godmother, tell me, pray do tell me, did mama die on my birthday?" . . .

Her darkened face had such power over me, that it stopped me in the midst of my vehemence. . . .

"Your mother, Esther, is your disgrace, and you were hers. . . . Forget your mother and leave all other people to forget her who will do her unhappy child that greatest kindness. Now go!"

She checked me, however, as I was about to depart from her—so frozen as I was!—and added this:

"Submission, self-denial, diligent work, are the preparations for a life begun with such a shadow on it. You are different from other children, Esther, because you were not born, like them, in common sinfulness and wrath. You are set apart." . . .

It must have been two years afterwards, and I was almost fourteen, when one dreadful night my godmother and I sat at the fireside. I was reading aloud, and she was listening. . . . [I] was reading, from St. John, how our Saviour stooped down, writing with his finger in the dust, when they brought the sinful woman to him.

" 'So when they continued asking him, he lifted up himself and said unto them, He that is without sin among you, let him first cast a stone at her!' "

I was stopped short by my godmother's rising, putting her hand to her head, and crying out, in an awful voice, from quite another part of the book:

" 'Watch ye therefore! lest coming suddenly he find you sleeping. And what I say unto you, I say unto all, Watch!' "

In an instant, while she stood before me repeating these words, she fell down upon the floor. I had no need to cry out; her voice had sounded through the house, and been heard in the street.

Various things in these two episodes recall Lady Dedlock's happening to recognize Captain Hawdon's handwriting. In both Esther is sitting with her godmother before the fire. In both reading is involved, though in the first it is only the reading of Miss Barbary's face. Writing is mentioned in the second, for Christ is "writing with his finger in the dust." In the first episode, Esther simply "happens" to look up at that moment at her godmother, and what she sees moves her to ask an impulsive question. She is given no real reply and her godmother's darkened face stops her "in the midst of [her] vehemence." After she is given the only answer Miss Barbary is willing to tell her, she is again "checked" and "frozen," recalling Lady Dedlock's "freezing mood." In the second scene, it is Miss Barbary who is so disturbed by what is read to her (the story of the woman taken in adultery in John 8:7) that she swoons, and indeed soon dies:

> She was laid upon her bed. For more than a week she lay there, little altered outwardly; with her old handsome resolute frown that I so well knew, carved upon her face. Many and many a time, in the day and in the night, with my head upon the pillow by her that my whispers might be plainer to her, I kissed her, thanked her, prayed for her, asked her for her bless-ing and forgiveness, entreated her to give me the least sign that she knew or heard me. No, no, no. Her face was immoveable. To the very last, and even afterwards, her frown remained unsoft-ened.

Miss Barbary's "old handsome resolute frown," her "carved" and "immoveable" features and her absolute unresponsiveness combine features of Lady Dedlock's "freezing mood," Esther's doll, and the Chancellor, who is "legally ignorant of [the man from Shropshire's] existence after making it desolate for a quarter of a century" (1). Indeed, Esther here is precisely in the position of Miss Flite, "the little mad old woman" who expects "some incomprehensible judgment," [14] and the quotation with which Esther's godmother counters her reading from St. John in fact foretells the Day of Judgment (Mark 13:35–37).

More important than the resonance with Miss Flite, how-ever, is the structural similarity between these scenes with Esther's godmother and the scene between the woman who is her real mother and Mr. Tulkinghorn. And as we shall see, the connections the texts asks us to make, indeed, even imposes on us, are important precisely because there is no real connection

36

in plot established between them at this point in the novel: the connections are merely, or purely, structural.

One further detail should link these scenes, and that is the reappearance just after Miss Barbary's death of "the gentleman in black" who had called on Esther two years before, just as Mr. Tulkinghorn, another gentleman in black, has called on Lady Dedlock. Mr. Kenge does not begin, as Mr. Tulkinghorn had, with a repetition of the words with which the novel had opened, "In Chancery." But he does almost as well: "our young friend," he says of Esther, "has no doubt heard of—the—a—Jarndyce and Jarndyce." Here the first real connection in plot between Esther's narrative and the first two chapters is apparent, although precisely what the connection is long remains secret.

With Esther's removal to Greenleaf under the secret guardianship of a party in Jarndyce and Jarndyce, she enjoys "six quiet years," she tells us, of respite from a world that the reader has by now come to know as "Chancery." But the respite ends with a summons from Kenge and Carboy to London. In fact, Esther returns to Chancery on the "same mirey afternoon" described in the first two chapters. The temporal circle begun with Esther's story of her early years has closed, and at precisely the same moment that the third-person narrator is guiding us through the public side of Chancery, Esther is hidden away with Richard Carstone and Ada Clare in the Chancellor's private room.

With Esther's arrival in court, the interrupted thread of events in the first chapter is at last taken up again and the novel may finally be said to have gotten under way. But Esther's experience of Chancery of course duplicates the picture of it in the opening chapter, so that even while we feel that at last we are moving forward we are also aware of having returned to the beginning and of still being in a state of animation-in-suspension. Esther writes of waiting in Mr. Kenge's office:

> Everything was so strange—the stranger from its being night in the day-time, the candles burning with a white flame, and looking raw and cold—that I read the words in the newspaper without knowing what they meant, and found myself reading the same words repeatedly. As it was no use going on in that way, I put the paper down, took a peep at my bonnet in the glass to see if it was neat, and looked at the room which was not half lighted . . . and at a bookcase full of the most inexpressive-looking books that ever had anything to say for themselves. Then I went on, thinking, thinking, thinking; and the fire went on, burning, burning, burning; and the candles went on flickering and guttering, and there were no snuffers—until the young gentleman by-and-by brought a very dirty pair; for two hours.

At this point the two narratives have perfectly linked up, for they are describing precisely the same things from two different points of view. They are describing not only a particular world, but our experience of that world. Like Esther, we read the words of the novel without quite knowing what they mean (that is, without yet knowing how they relate to one another), and find ourselves reading what amount to the same words repeatedly. But from this point on, the two narratives split up again, and though they overlap almost entirely in regard to the characters they encompass, they will not come to describe the same events again (except, occasionally, at second-hand) until chapters 56 and 57 (at the juncture of numbers 17 and 18) where Esther takes up the search for Lady Dedlock at exactly the moment when the third person narrator leaves off.

SUSPENDED ANIMATION

In a sense it is here that the novel's prelude ends and the action of the novel proper begins, but in saying this I am also choosing a somewhat arbitrary point, for in the following chapter, the last of the opening number, we are presented with the Jellyby family and material that is at once new to us and familiar. Mrs. Jellyby's home obviously mirrors the chaos of Chancery. Her room is "strewn with papers and nearly filled by a great writing-table covered with similar litter," reminiscent of "the registrar's red table . . . with bills, cross-bills, answers, rejoinders, injunctions, affidavits, issues, references to masters, masters' reports, mountains of costly nonsense, piled before [the Chancery solicitors]" as well as Miss Flite's "small litter . . . which she calls her documents" (1). But beyond this there does not seem at first to be any connection between Mrs. Jellyby's philanthropic activities and Chancery. Mrs. Jellyby's world clearly has little use for "precedent and usage" and her plan to place "two hundred healthy families cultivating coffee and educating the natives of Borrioboola-Gha, on the left bank of the Niger" would seem as far removed from Chancery as it is possible to be. Nevertheless, Dickens links Chancery and Mrs. Jellyby's philanthropic schemes by pointing out that they share a central notion, the idea of a "cause." Being in a cause or having a cause is the one thing that unites the worlds of the Jellybys, Chancery, the Dedlocks, and indeed everyone in the opening number. Exploring the meaning of that idea and tracing its implications is a task that will take Dickens the whole rest of the novel to accomplish, but we are already in a position to make some generalizations about the novel based upon our reading of the opening number.

SUSPENDED ANIMATION

III

Concerning the opening chapters of *Bleak House* Hillis Miller writes:

> The narrative line of *Bleak House* shifts continually from one space-time to another apparently simultaneous with it but otherwise unconnected. It is not until we are far into the novel that relations between widely separated actions and milieus begin to appear. At first it seems that Dickens, inexplicably, has chosen to write two or three novels at once, and to alternate with no apparent rhyme or reason from portraits of the aristocratic world of Lady Dedlock at Chesney Wold to the very different stories of Esther Summerson and the wards in Jarndyce. Moreover, a great number of minor characters are presented who have no obvious relation to the major stories.[15]

This would be true if by "relations" we meant only fully understood causal relations. But of course this is not all that "relations" means. The one thing we do know about all the events and characters in *Bleak House*'s opening number is that they are related because they are all involved in the same kind of suspended animation and the same kind of inhibited or circular activity. Indeed, it is just because the causal relations between these people and events are not from the outset understood that the relations between them are perceived virtually as identity. This is the force of the mirroring of the different worlds we are shown at the novel's beginning. To hold causal relationships in suspension and to portray a series of worlds which share a number of overlapping attributes and details prevents us from making any clear discriminations between them, and tends rather to make us see reflections even where no obvious over-

40

lapping exists. The invocation of the world of fairy-tales in relation to the fashionable world at the beginning of the second
chapter, for example, does not serve to distinguish the world of
fashion from that of Chancery, which has its reference in the
cosmologies of the Bible, Milton, and Victorian geology, but
instead adds another kind of legendary framework relevant to
Chancery. And the converse is true, though at this point in the
novel (in chapter 2) we can know this only semiconsciously or
implicitly by allowing our imagination to give free rein to the
mirroring of the two worlds. Only later in the novel will the
religious and geological aspects of the fashionable world be explicitly revealed (for example, in the discussion of religious
"Dandyism" [12] or the geological references to Chesney Wold
and the Dedlocks discussed above).

The insistent mirroring of the novel's worlds (conveyed in
the specific train of mirror imagery in the novel as well as in its
general structure) not only tends to make for the identification
or confusion of all these worlds but also paradoxically provides
Dickens with a device whereby he can prepare us for the important "revelations" in the rest of the novel. If we look for causal
relationships in the novel's opening number, we shall not find
them, and the novel will indeed appear, as Miller suggests, to
be made up of unrelated people and events. If, however, we
relax our conscious search for such relations, and allow the tendency for separate people and events to fuse—if, in other words,
we give ourselves up to the confusion of *Bleak House,* then we
will find that no event in the novel can come as a true surprise
to us; rather every "new" development will strike us with a sense
at once of familiarity and inevitability.

Let us take, as an example one of the central mysteries in

the novel, the question of Esther's identity. What really do we learn about it in the opening number? In terms of hard evidence, almost nothing. We are led to believe that she is an orphan, and illegitimate. We know that her guardian is Mr. Jarndyce and that he is in a Chancery suit, but we have no way of knowing how he came to be her guardian. Nevertheless, if we allow the parallels between Esther and Lady Dedlock as evidence of another kind, we shall find that we know a great deal. The obvious parallels are primarily between the scene in which Lady Dedlock recognizes the handwriting of the manuscript Tulkinghorn reads to her, and the scene on Esther's birthday and her reading to her godmother, as well as the intervening visit of Mr. Kenge. We are told that Lady Dedlock is childless, and we sense that her childlessness is at the root of her being put "quite out of temper" and the mask of boredom that conceals her uneasiness. But we also know that Lady Dedlock has a secret—perhaps having a connection with Jarndyce and Jarndyce, but in any case one whose hold over her is so strong that the mere sight of a particular handwriting is enough to make this grand woman fairly swoon. We know that Miss Barbary holds a similar secret, also one that is possibly connected with Jarndyce and Jarndyce, and also one whose hold over *her* is so great that simply hearing the story of Jesus writing in the dust and being presented with the woman taken in adultery is enough not only to make her swoon but in fact to kill her, though her characteristic resolute and handsome composure is as firm as Lady Dedlock's. We might also suspect that Miss Barbary's secret has to do with Esther's identity, for several reasons, but most clearly because of the parallel between the biblical story and Esther's illegitimate birth. Dickens places just one serious obstacle in the way of our causally connecting Lady Dedlock and Miss Barbary and Esther, and realizing that Lady Dedlock and Miss Barbary are sisters in fact as well as in spirit, and that is our supposition that Lady Dedlock is childless and that Esther is an orphan—although the latter is ambiguous.

That we are prepared for every event in the novel of course does not mean that we are conscious of that preparation, for the parallels between images, characters, or events are generally drawn by references to apparently indifferent common denominators which are veiled because they appear in successively different contexts. Thus, when we learn that Mrs. Jellyby is devoted to a philanthropic "cause" (4) we probably shall not consciously connect her cause with Chancery causes, because the everyday sense of the language selects for us quite different meanings for the word in these two contexts. Nevertheless, it is through such delicate punning that we can pinpoint the relatedness of the Jellybys and Chancery and that we can understand that both worlds have their reference in the idea of a "cause" not only in its various particular senses, but in its most general and abstract sense. We have already seen this kind of punning in the circle of words with overlapping meanings that Esther constructs to describe the anxious confusions of her childhood. It is a confusion that not coincidentally is expressed by the relative absence of causal (that is, logical) relationships in her thoughts and indeed is explicitly about her failure to understand her own causal relations with the world—"What did I do to [my mother]?" she asks Miss Barbary, "How did I lose her? Why am I so different from other children, and why is it my fault, dear godmother?" (3). Though Esther does not use the word "cause" here, nevertheless she is implicitly carrying on the elaborate play on the word that has begun in the first chapter with "the cause" of Jarndyce and Jarndyce and that in many ways forms the novel's real subject or asks the central question—"Where do I come from?" It is, of course, the most basic question that we can ask about ourselves, and the question our most basic myths seek to answer.

Bleak House is about "causes" and "relations" in every conceivable meaning and combination of meanings of those two words. It begins, we should recall, with a picture of causal relationships that have been entirely dislocated and turned upside down. This is the especial horror of Chaos, and this too is what makes the pun the most important device by which we can understand or make connections within the world of the novel, for it is in the very nature of puns that they can be intuitively understood without one's consciously making the logical connections between their various meanings. And it is this fact that makes the suspense of the opening number not only bearable, but pleasurable. The mirroring of the novel's various worlds and the tendency to see reflections even where there is no explicit overlapping of details (itself a kind of punning on a grand scale) is just what allows us, in spite of all the apparent discontinuity in the first four chapters, to know, if only at the back of our minds, that indeed the connections exist, and that Lady Dedlock and Esther are related by the profoundest of ties.

The circular patterns I have been tracing in *Bleak House*'s opening number are of course not perfectly circular: things do not repeat themselves with exactness, but rather with variation. When Esther's narrative catches up with that of the third-person narrator, we find ourselves almost exactly where we had been left at the end of the first chapter, but not quite: only a door separates us from our former selves. As skillful as Dickens is in maintaining his circles, he is equally skillful in playing out his variations—variations sometimes so complex as to all but hide from us the fact that we have moved in circles. The experience for the reader is thus one of *déjà vu*. We are continually being made to feel that we have been here before while at the same time we know that we have not, and this is especially the case in those scenes which structurally and dynamically echo previous ones without there being a manifest connection (generally in plot) between them. It is this circular experience of *déjà vu* (doubly circular, really, for it is circular in itself and circular in that it is itself repeated) that represents for me a kind of continual peripety and that represents for me further one structural embodiment of Dickens's dwelling "on the romantic side of familiar things." Peripety means of course literally "a falling round"; what we have seen in the beginning of *Bleak House* is a falling round and round and round, and one that continually makes the familiar strange and the strange familiar.

This is precisely the experience we have already seen described by Esther as she waits for the Chancellor in the passage I have taken as my epigraph, and it is an experience that is not restricted to the labyrinthine world of Chancery, but one that pervades even the relatively secure worlds of *Bleak House*. Indeed, it pervades Bleak House (the house) itself, as Esther tells us in describing it in the next number, for "you might,' if you came out at another door [of Mr. Jarndyce's room] (every room had at least two doors), go straight down to the hall again by half-a-dozen steps and a low archway, wondering how you got back there, or had ever got out of it" (6). [16] But this gets us into the subject of my next chapter.

CHAPTER THREE

BLEAK HOUSE, II
THE UNCANNY

"Is there three *of 'em then?"*
—*Jo, Chapter 31*

I

EVERYONE knows about Dickens's "imagination." And almost everyone agrees that it was in his imagination that Dickens's genius dwelt. Even those critics who have found Dickens wanting in intellect, education, and artistry have almost unanimously praised his imagination; indeed, one sometimes suspects that such praise is there simply to underscore other deficiencies, and in the mouths of some critics the phrase "imaginative genius" is apt to sound like "natural fool." But the silliness of such attitudes aside, everyone, again, agrees on the richness of his imagination, so much so that it has become the favorite subject, explicit or implicit, of modern critical studies.[1]

The Dickens imagination manifests itself, of course, in an extraordinarily large number of ways, but the way that has been chiefly remarked by the critics, from very early on, is the way of a vividness of perception so intense as to be virtually hallucina-

47

THE UNCANNY

tory. G. H. Lewes's formulation in his famous essay written shortly after Dickens's death is one of the first and most widely known:

> Of him it may be said with less exaggeration than of most poets, that he was of "imagination all compact"; if the other higher faculties were singularly deficient in him, this faculty was imperial. He was a seer of visions; and his visions were of objects at once familiar and potent. Psychologists will understand both the extent and the limitation of the remark, when I say that in no other perfectly sane mind (Blake, I believe, was not perfectly sane) have I observed vividness of imagination approaching so closely to hallucination. . . . When he imagined a street, a house, a room, a figure, he saw it not in the vague schematic way of ordinary imagination, but in the sharp definition of actual perception, all the salient details obtruding themselves on his attention. He, seeing it thus vividly, made us also see it; and believing in its reality, however fantastic, he communicated something of his belief to us. He presented it in such relief that we ceased to think of it as a picture. So definite and insistent was the image, that even while knowing it was false we could not help, for a moment, being affected, as it were, by his hallucination.[2]

This hallucinatory vividness of perception, which is the normal condition of Dickens's prose, is of course closely allied with his lifetime interest in frankly sensational and abnormal psychology. Two years after Lewes's essay, R. H. Hutton wrote of Dickens that

> No author indeed could draw more powerfully than he the mood of a man haunted by a fixed idea, a shadowy apprehen-

48

sion, a fear, a dream, a remorse. If Dickens had to describe the restlessness of a murderer, or the panic of a man apprehending murder, he did it with a vigour and force that make the blood curdle. But there, again, he was studying in a world of most specific experience. He was a vivid dreamer, and no one knew better the sort of supremacy which a given idea gets over the mind in a dream, and in those waking states of nervous apprehension akin to dreams.[3]

The truth of such observations as Lewes's and Hutton's account in part for the waning of Dickens's reputation in the last quarter of the nineteenth century and the revival of critical interest in him in the twentieth (popular interest never having waned) as a psychological, anti-realist (even surrealist) novelist, one who invites comparison with Dostoevsky, Joyce, and Kafka. Edmund Wilson's classic essay "Dickens: The Two Scrooges" (1939) in particular takes up where Lewes and Hutton leave off. The advance that has been made over the past century in exploring either the hallucinatory quality of the prose or the interest in abnormal psychology has not been great, however. The most interesting extended study is Taylor Stoehr's *Dickens: The Dreamer's Stance* (Ithaca: Cornell University Press, 1965), which finds in the novels the same structures and dynamics Freud was later to discover in dreams: the grammar of psychoanalytic dream-interpretation thus becomes a useful grammar for literary criticism. Steven Marcus has brilliantly examined Oliver Twist's hypnagogic reveries in connection with Dickens's life in his appendix to *Dickens: From Pickwick to Dombey* (New York: Basic Books, 1965), but the findings in his essay have for some reason unhappily resisted assimilation into the canon of Dickens studies, just as they remain detached from the body of his book. J. Hillis Miller's work is most definitely, and in some ways exclusively, about the Dickens "imagination," and yet in *Charles Dickens: The World of His Novels* he rigorously avoids explicit mention of all psychological categories: only in "The Fiction of Realism" have they begun tentatively to sneak in.

We have, I think, already learned enough about how *Bleak House*'s opening number works and about how the imagination that conceived it works to begin to refine some of the Dickens critics' formulations about the Dickens "imagination." Certainly we have seen that the opening number is hallucinatory and dreamlike enough, but we should also by now have come to see that such descriptions embrace only half of the paradox: they suggest the "romantic side" but not the "familiar." What we have seen, rather, is that throughout the opening number and in a host of ways Dickens has maintained a kind of continual unsettling peripety or double perspective, the effect of which is to establish a constant tension between all of those polarities evoked by the "romantic" and the "familiar": the strange and the familiar, the eternal and the topical, the dreaming and the waking, and so on. And the best example of this tension is I think the experience I touched upon at the end of the last chapter, the experience of imperfect, circular, and involuntary repetition we know as *déjà vu*.

Perhaps the single most intense and unsettling experience of *déjà vu* in the novel belongs to Jo, the crossing-sweeper. In the delirium of fever, he mistakes Esther at once for Lady Dedlock (whom he has met in chapter 16) and Mlle. Hortense (whom he has met in chapter 22 through a contrived restaging of the earlier scene by Mr. Tulkinghorn and Mr. Bucket), and in a moment of terror is faced with the triple paradox of three

THE UNCANNY

women who are at once the same and not the same—who are doubles of one another:

> I had not lifted my veil [Esther writes] when I first spoke to the woman, which was at the moment of our going in. The boy staggered up instantly, and stared at me with a remarkable expression of surprise and terror.
>
> His action was so quick, and my being the cause of it was so evident, that I stood still, instead of advancing nearer.
>
> "I won't go no more to the berryin ground," muttered the boy; "I ain't a-going there, so I tell you!"
>
> I lifted my veil and spoke to the woman. She said to me in a low voice, "Don't mind him, ma'am. He'll soon come back to his head;" and said to him, "Jo, Jo, what's the matter?"
>
> "I know wot she's come for!" cried the boy.
>
> "Who?"
>
> "The lady there. She's come to get me to go along with her to the berryin ground. I won't go to the berryin ground. I don't like the name on it. She might go a-berryin *me.*" His shivering came on again, and as he leaned against the wall, he shook the hovel.
>
> "He has been talking off and on about such like, all day, ma'am," said Jenny, softly. "Why, how you stare! This is *my* lady, Jo."
>
> "Is it?" returned the boy, doubtfully, and surveying me with his arm held out above his burning eyes. "She looks to me the t'other one. . . . I say!" said the boy [to Charley]. "*You* tell me. Ain't the lady the t'other lady?"
>
> Charley shook her head, as she methodically drew his rags about him and made him as warm as she could.
>
> "O!" the boy muttered. "Then I suppose she ain't. . . .
>
> "If she ain't the t'other one, she ain't the forrenner. Is there *three* of 'em then?"
>
> Charley looked at me a little frightened. I felt half frightened at myself when the boy glared on me so. (31)

THE UNCANNY

Jo's horrifying experience of *déjà vu* here is hardly unique, however. Indeed, it is but the climactic instance of a series of experiences of *déjà vu* connected with Esther that have begun in the novel's second number with Guppy's happening to see the portrait of lady Dedlock during his tour of Chesney Wold:

> Even the long drawing-room of Chesney Wold cannot revive Mr. Guppy's spirits. He is so low that he droops on the threshold, and has hardly strength of mind to enter. But a portrait over the chimney-piece, painted by the fashionable artist of the day, acts upon him like a charm. He recovers in a moment. He stares at it with uncommon interest; he seems to be fixed and fascinated by it.
>
> "Dear me!" says Mr. Guppy. "Who's that?"
>
> "The picture over the fire-place," says Rosa, "is the portrait of the present Lady Dedlock. It is considered a perfect likeness, and the best work of the master."
>
> "Blest!" says Mr. Guppy, staring in a kind of dismay at his friend, "if I can ever have seen her. Yet I know her! . . . It's unaccountable to me," he says, still staring at the portrait, "how well I know that picture! I'm dashed!" adds Mr. Guppy, looking round, "if I don't think I must have had a dream of that picture, you know!"
>
> As no one present takes any interest in Mr. Guppy's dreams, the probability is not pursued. But he still remains so absorbed by the portrait, that he stands immoveable before it until the young gardener has closed the shutters; when he comes out of the room in a dazed state, that is an odd though a sufficient substitute for interest, and follows into the succeeding rooms with a confused stare, as if he were looking everywhere for Lady Dedlock again. (7)

Of course Guppy is confusing Lady Dedlock's image with Esther's, though as yet he has made no conscious connection between them. And Mr. George, who has grown up at Chesney Wold and knows Lady Dedlock's features well, has a similar experience on first meeting Esther. She writes:

> If [Mr. George] had not looked at me before, he looked at me now, in three or four quick successive glances. "I beg your pardon, sir," he said to my guardian, with a manly kind of diffidence, "but you did me the honour to mention the young lady's name——"
> "Miss Summerson."
> "Miss Summerson," he repeated, and looked at me again.
> "Do you know the name?" I asked.
> "No, miss. To my knowledge, I never heard of it. I thought I had seen you somewhere."
> "I think not," I returned, raising my head from my work to look at him; and there was something so genuine in his speech and manner that I was glad of the opportunity. "I remember faces very well."
> "So do I, miss!" he returned, meeting my look with the fulness of his dark eyes and broad forehead. "Humph! What set me off, now, upon that!" (24)

But Esther's being the repeated object of an experience of *déjà vu* is merely the most prominent such case in the novel, and the experience of *déjà vu* is a common one for the characters in *Bleak House*, especially if we include within its range incidents in which the experience proves to be not illusory, but true. They begin with the second day of the novel, when Richard, Ada and Esther happen upon Miss Flite for the second time:

> "So cousin," said the cheerful voice of Richard to Ada, behind me. "We are never to get out of Chancery! We have come by another way to our place of meeting yesterday, and—by the Great Seal, here's the old lady again!"

THE UNCANNY

> Truly, there she was, immediately in front of us, curtseying,
> and smiling, and saying, with her yesterday's air of patronage:
> "The wards in Jarndyce! Ve-ry happy, I am sure!" (5)

It is Richard's little joke that "we are never to get out of Chancery" that strikes an eerie note and warns us that the coincidence here involves precisely that sort of involuntary repetition that has been familiar to the reader from the novel's first page.

It is finally we, the readers, for whom the experience of *déjà vu* is most persistent, inasmuch as we participate in the experience of all the characters and have in addition been provided with a series of such experiences all our own. Nothing demonstrates this more clearly than a feature peculiar to the novel's most prominent example of double perspective, that of the double narrative. We are familiar with Dickens's habit, as early as *Pickwick Papers*, of introducing characters who drop out of sight for long stretches of a novel, only to be reintroduced later on, often in semi-disguised fashion. The reappearance of Mr. Jingle and Job Trotter after an absence of almost twenty chapters (*Pickwick*, 25 and 42), is a good example. In *Bleak House*, Dickens pushes this device to its limits—since there are several characters who drop out for long stretches—and he adds an entirely new dimension to it by virtue of the double narrative. There are in *Bleak House* about a hundred characters (an average number for a full-length Dickens novel). Of these, roughly a third could be called significant (again a typical figure) and, with only a handful of exceptions, it is these thirty or so who figure in both narratives. Now what this means is that we are introduced to all of these characters, *as though for the first time*, twice. That makes for a grand total of almost a hundred and forty introductions. And they are much more evenly spaced throughout the novel than we might expect. In fact, I count only thirty-six (out of sixty-seven) chapters in which we are *not* introduced to one of the novel's significant characters. Thus, Esther is still meeting characters for the first time who have long been familiar to us from the third-person narrative towards the very end of the novel. She does not meet the Snagsbys, for example, until chapter 59, and it is later still that she first sees the Smallweeds (62) and Tony Jobling (64). Matters are made even more complicated by the fact that we sometimes reencounter a character previously introduced but now in disguise—Lady Dedlock, for example, when she goes on her tour of Nemo's haunts and burying-ground (16), or Mr. Bucket when he appears disguised as an old physician at Mr. George's shooting-gallery to arrest Gridley (24). And the full introduction of other characters extends over a series of meetings. We first see Allan Woodcourt as the "dark young" doctor who mysteriously appears at Nemo's deathbed at the beginning of number four (11). His appearance out of nowhere and his being unnamed are themselves strange enough.[4] He is introduced again at the very end of the number by Esther as "a gentleman of a dark complexion—a young surgeon" (13) who had dined with her at the Bayham Badgers', but he is still unnamed, and not connected with the physician who had attended at Nemo's death (though of course the similarity in description and the symmetry of his appearances, at the very beginning and end of the same monthly number, should give us a clue). In the following chapter (14), we at last meet Mr. Woodcourt, named as the doctor who has been caring for Miss Flite since her fright at Nemo's death, and identified as the doctor who had examined Nemo. But Esther waits until the very end of the chapter—until a sort of postscript to it, in fact—to identify him further as the physician who had dined with her at the Badgers': "I have forgotten to mention," she writes, "—at least I have not mentioned—that Mr. Woodcourt was the same dark young surgeon whom we had met at Mr. Badger's."

The mysteriousness and prolongation of Mr. Woodcourt's introduction to us can of course be accounted for as an instance of Esther's coyness about a young man for whom she has obviously felt a strong attraction from the very first. But we should note how well Esther's coyness fits in here with Dickens's desire to reproduce or anticipate in the reader, even if in somewhat milder form, the kind of experience Jo has in first meeting Esther. At the point that we are introduced to Allan Woodcourt as Miss Flite's doctor, we feel perfectly justified in believing that we have just been introduced to three distinct young doctors, and though our suspicions have by this point no doubt been aroused, we might very well ask with Jo, "Is there *three* of 'em then?" And the point is not so much whether there are in reality three (as there are in the case of Mlle. Hortense, Lady Dedlock, and Esther) or only one (as in the case of Allan Woodcourt), but rather that the question has been raised at all. What is going on here is exactly what has been going on from the novel's first page. We are continually being led to believe that we are meeting people, or entering places, or witnessing events, that are new and unfamiliar to us, only to discover that what we are seeing as though for the first time is nothing new at all, but something old and familiar.

II

These are almost exactly the words Freud uses in his great essay on *déjà vu* and all those other phenomena he groups together under the heading of the "uncanny," which is, he writes, "in reality nothing new or alien, but something familiar and old-established in the mind that has become alienated from it only through the process of repression." [5] That statement should put us in mind again of "the romantic side of familiar things," and suggests to me further that it is towards the class of phenomena Freud discusses as uncanny that we should look in refining the traditional views of Dickens's writing as hallucinatory and dreamlike.

Freud lists in his essay, besides *déjà vu*, such things as inanimate objects which seem to be alive (and vice versa), haunted houses, repeated coincidences, repetitions (if they are insistent enough) of any kind, telepathy, various manifestations of epilepsy, and hypnosis. We have by now seen that the first four items in this list figure importantly in *Bleak House*, and we shall presently see that from the whole list nothing in fact can be excepted as playing no significant role in the novel; but for the moment let us have a look at what Freud has to say about the uncanny in general.

As is so often his strategy, Freud begins his essay by looking to the dictionary and the common language, which, as he says elsewhere, "is no chance thing, but the precipitate of old discoveries." [6] "The *unheimlich* [uncanny] is what was once *heimisch* [homey], familiar; the prefix '*un*' ['un-'] is the token of repression." [7] But we do not need to revert to the German to understand his point, for the English "uncanny" and "canny" interestingly reproduce an almost exact correspondence with the meaning and relationship between the two words in German—even though they derive from words with quite different meanings. Following the *Oxford English Dictionary*, the most common meaning of the Scotch "canny" is "Careful or cautious in motion or action: *hence*, quiet, gentle, 'soft' of speech; free from commotion, disturbance, or noise." But the word, though apparently derived from "can" (as a verb, meaning "to know how, be able"), and in its earliest sense meaning something very close to "cunning," also has precisely the meaning of the German *heimlich*, i.e., "Quiet, easy, snug, comfortable, pleasant, cosy" and "Lucky or safe to meddle with." It is easy to see that these are the senses that are reversed in "uncanny," becoming "Mischievous, malicious," "Careless, incautious," "Unreliable, not to be trusted," "Of persons: Not quite safe to trust to, or have dealings with, as being associated with supernatural arts or powers" and finally, "Partaking of a supernatural character; mysterious, weird, uncomfortably strange or unfamiliar." (This last meaning, today by far the most common, does not in fact appear in the language until the middle of the last century—that is, just at the time *Bleak House* was being written.) And just as the German *heimlich* can also mean its opposite, so too can the English "canny," which has (or had, rather, for this sense dropped out of the language at the beginning of the last century) the additional sense of being "Supernaturally wise, endowed with occult or magical power." And a further, more narrow meaning of *heimlich*, of particular interest to Freud, and derived from its meaning of "secret" or "private," i.e., the *"heimlich* parts of the human body, *pudenda*," [8] also has its counterpart, if not a near equivalent, in the now obsolete Scotch "canny-wife" and "canny moment," meaning "midwife" and "moment of birth," respectively.

It is significant, I think, and considerably strengthens Freud's case that even though the German and English words are of entirely different derivation, they have come to denote such closely associated attributes. Thus the English "canny," originally having nothing to do with the idea of the home, does come to have homey associations, while the German *heimlich*, originally having nothing to do with the idea of knowledge, eventually is used in connection with knowledge, as in the phrase *heimlich räthe*, meaning privy councilors or officials "who give important advice which has to be kept secret." [9]

The constellation of meanings for both *unheimlich* and "canny" is strikingly similar—I am tempted to say uncannily similar—to *Bleak House*'s major themes and subjects. The similarity is apparent first of all in the novel's title, which certainly suggests an unhomey house, even an unhousely house, and thus contains within itself precisely the antithesis of this constellation of meanings. The similarity becomes inescapable when we consider how deeply the novel is concerned with houses and their relative bleakness and homeyness. Dickens, almost as though he had his dictionary open at "canny" before him, describes all the many houses of *Bleak House* as either quiet, cosy, orderly, and safe, or as careless, noisy, unsafe and even haunted. All of the novel's houses, like Bleak House itself, have both "canny" and "uncanny" qualities in varying degrees, and all of them are haunted, [10] but the point again is that it is this particular constellation of qualities that Dickens chooses to specify and dramatize.

The significance of Dickens's interest in the "canny" and the "uncanny" (or the homey and the unhomey) should be generally clear. The great lesson of *Bleak House* of course (though twentieth-century critics are apt to evade it) is that Charity (and Justice and most virtues, indeed) begins at Home. Chancery is as much an instance of Telescopic Philanthropy and as much an instance of bad parenthood and careless domestic arrangements—it legally serves both as surrogate parent and as surrogate landlord—as Mrs. Jellyby's Borrioboolan project and home. Esther's whole "Progress" is a demonstration of what Dickens believes to be the literal truth of the doctrine, and her implicit rebuke to Mrs. Pardiggle, "I thought it best to be as useful as I could . . . to those immediately about me; and to try to let that circle of duty gradually and naturally expand itself" (8), both expresses the doctrine and suggests its less obvious relevance to Chancery, to whose "circle of . . . evil" (1) Esther's "circle of duty" is clearly meant to be opposed. And thus it is always centrally the "canny" Esther who brings relative quiet, cosiness, orderliness, and safety to the houses she lives in and visits. Indeed, of all the houses she visits, the only one that resists absolutely her influence is Harold Skimpole's, and he of course is Esther's most conscious and absolute opposite in the novel.

Toward the end of the last chapter, I suggested that the great subject of *Bleak House* was the idea of "causal relations" in all possible meanings of that phrase, and that raises a question: What is the connection between the subject and the lesson? What does an elaborate examination of "causal relations" have to do with the doctrine that Charity begins at Home? It is too early to offer a perfectly satisfactory answer, and perhaps a perfectly satisfactory answer will ultimately elude us; but for the moment, let me suggest the direction in which we should look for an answer by pointing out that to answer that question would also probably answer another question I have raised in comparing the words "canny" and *heimlich:* how is it that a word having originally to do with unusual knowledge and ability and closely related to "cunning" and "ken" [11] comes to mean "homey," while a word in another language and of entirely separate derivation originally meaning "homey" comes to denote special and secret knowledge? What, in other words, is the exact association of ideas that relates the history of the words "canny" and *heimlich*, and reappears as an organizing body of associations in *Bleak House*?

Freud offers an implicit answer in discussing the specifically sexual sense of *heimlich* as it is used to describe the secret parts of the body, the genitalia—the sense of *heimlich* that has its counterpart in the Scotch "canny-wife" and "canny moment." Freud writes:

> It often happens that neurotic men declare that they feel there is something uncanny about the female genital organs. This *unheimlich* place, however, is the entrance to the former *Heim* [home] of all human beings, to the place where each one of us lived once upon a time and in the beginning. There is a joking saying that 'Love is home-sickness'; and whenever a man dreams of a place or a country and says to himself, while he is still dreaming: "this place is familiar to me, I have been there before," we may interpret the place as being his mother's genitals or her body. In this case, too, then, the *unheimlich* is what was once *heimisch*, familiar; the prefix 'un' ['un-'] is the token of repression. [12]

Inasmuch as a large part of *Bleak House* is about the secret of Esther's identity, we can say that it is about how the identity of Esther's first "home" has been "repressed" and made strange to her. She in fact has an intense experience of *déjà vu* when she visits Chesney Wold and first sees her mother:

Shall I ever forget the rapid beating at my heart, occasioned by the look I met, as I stood up! Shall I ever forget the manner in which those handsome proud eyes seemed to spring out of their languor, and to hold mine! It was only a moment before I cast mine down—released again, if I may say so—on my book; but, I knew the beautiful face quite well, in that short space of time.

And, very strangely, there was something quickened within me, associated with the lonely days at my godmother's; yes, away even to the days when I had stood on tiptoe to dress myself at my little glass, after dressing my doll. And thus, although I had never seen this lady's face before in all my life—I was quite sure of it—absolutely certain.

It was easy to know that the ceremonious, gouty, grey-haired gentleman, the only other occupant of the great pew, was Sir Leicester Dedlock; and that the lady was Lady Dedlock. But why her face should be, in a confused way, like a broken glass to me, in which I saw scraps of old remembrances; and why I should be so fluttered and troubled (for I was still), by having casually met her eyes; I could not think. (18)

Here the memory (or secret) that threatens to break out into consciousness is of course not mediated by the symbol of a house: it is Lady Dedlock's face (and its similarity to her sister Miss Barbary's and to Esther's own) that triggers the experience. But if we understand the connection Freud makes between houses and our first figurative home, then we can more easily see how Dickens's continual fascination with houses in *Bleak House* connects with the theme of "causal relations." The most basic causal questions we can ask ourselves, and the most difficult to answer—or, when answered, to accept—are "who am I?" and "where do I come from?" For Dickens, the question is often implicitly framed as "to what house do I belong?" Dick-

THE UNCANNY

ens's attraction to the "canny" domestic virtues thus signifies a good deal more than a weakness for the creature comforts; a "canny" home signifies for him rather that one has a secure place and a secure identity.

Esther has another experience of *déjà vu* in connection with her mother almost immediately after the one I have just quoted, and here not only do we share the feeling of *déjà vu*, but that feeling is evoked through the agency of a house, and a house, moreover, whose symbolic function is precisely the one Freud has outlined. Esther, Ada, and Mr. Jarndyce have been walking through the grounds of Chesney Wold when they are overtaken by a sudden summer thunderstorm and seek shelter in a keeper's lodge. Esther writes:

> We had often noticed the dark beauty of this lodge standing in a deep twilight of trees, and how the ivy clustered over it, and how there was a steep hollow near, where we had once seen the keeper's dog dive down into the fern as if it were water.
>
> The lodge was so dark within, now the sky was overcast, that we only clearly saw the man who came to the door when we took shelter there, and put two chairs for Ada and me. The lattice-windows were all thrown open, and we sat, just within the doorway, watching the storm. It was grand to see how the wind awoke, and bent the trees, and drove the rain before it like a cloud of smoke; and to hear the solemn thunder, and to see the lightning; and while thinking with awe of the tremendous powers by which our little lives are encompassed, to consider how beneficent they are, and how upon the smallest flower and leaf there was already a freshness poured from all this seeming rage, which seemed to make creation new again.
>
> "Is it not dangerous to sit in so exposed a place?"
> "O no, Esther dear!" said Ada, quietly.
> Ada said it to me; but *I* had not spoken.

63

THE UNCANNY

The beating of my heart came back again. I had never heard the voice, as I had never seen the face, but it affected me in the same strange way. Again, in a moment, there arose before my mind innumerable pictures of myself.

Lady Dedlock had taken shelter in the lodge, before our arrival there, and had come out of the gloom within. She stood behind my chair, with her hand upon it. I saw her with her hand close to my shoulder, when I turned my head. (18)

Here, of course, it is the resemblance between Lady Dedlock's voice and Esther's—clearly meant to be as striking as that between their looks—that arouses in Esther a feeling of uncanniness. We as readers of Esther's narrative certainly share her unsettling feelings, but for us there is an additional source of uncanny feeling here, a source that derives from something we have read long before in the other narrative, with our very first view of Lady Dedlock:

My Lady Dedlock (who is childless), looking out in the early twilight from her boudoir at a keeper's lodge, and seeing the light of a fire upon the latticed panes, and smoke rising from the chimney, and a child, chased by a woman, running out into the rain to meet the shining figure of a wrapped-up man coming through the gate, has been put quite out of temper. My Lady Dedlock says she has been "bored to death." (2)

For us, it is the keeper's lodge that triggers the feeling of uncanniness. This house we have seen long ago through Lady Dedlock's eyes (and that, no doubt, we are supposed to have since "forgotten") plainly points to Lady Dedlock's supposed childlessness. In fact, of course, it points to her motherhood, to the child she believes to be dead, to the father who has run away, and to the home they all might have lived in. [13]

THE UNCANNY

III

We may say, then, that *Bleak House* offers us essentially the same thematic concerns as are suggested by the history of the words "canny" and *heimlich*, and we should by now have some idea of what gives those concerns coherence. More interesting, perhaps, and more relevant to our understanding of "the romantic side of familiar things," is the resonance between Dickens's techniques for evoking feelings of uncanniness and Freud's description of the conditions that give rise to and the particular dynamics of the uncanny. Let us look at that description more closely.

Freud summarizes by saying that "an uncanny experience occurs either when infantile complexes which have been repressed are once more revived by some impression, or when primitive beliefs which have been surmounted [superstitions] seem once more to be confirmed," and he further notes that the differences between "these two classes of uncanny experience are not always sharply distinguishable," inasmuch as primitive beliefs are themselves based upon infantile complexes. [14] And he appends to his summary a brief discussion of the uncanny in literature, which, he says, provides "a much more fertile province than the uncanny in real life, for it contains the whole of the latter and something even more besides, something that cannot be found in real life." He continues:

> The imaginative writer has this licence among many others, that he can select his world of representation so that it either coincides with the realities we are familiar with or departs from them in what particulars he pleases. We accept his ruling in every case. In fairy tales, for instance, the world of reality is left behind from the very start, and the animistic system of beliefs is

frankly adopted. Wish-fulfillments, secret powers, omnipotence of thoughts, animation of inanimate objects, all the elements so common in fairy stories, can exert no uncanny influence here; for, as we have learnt, that feeling cannot arise unless there is a conflict of judgement as to whether things which have been "surmounted" and are regarded as incredible may not, after all, be possible; and this problem is eliminated from the outset by the postulates of the world of fairy tales.

The situation is altered as soon as the writer pretends to move in the world of common reality. In this case he accepts as well all the conditions operating to produce uncanny feelings in real life; and everything that would have an uncanny effect in reality has it in his story. But in this case, he can even increase his effect and multiply it far beyond what would happen in reality, by bringing about events which never or very rarely happen in fact. In doing this he is in a sense betraying us to the superstitiousness which we have ostensibly surmounted; he deceives us by promising to give us the sober truth, and then after all overstepping it. We react to his inventions as we would have reacted to real experiences; by the time we have seen through his trick it is already too late and the author has achieved his object. . . .[15]

Freud is speaking of course of those works which belong to the genre of the horror story, to which *Bleak House*, properly speaking, does not. But it is clear too that the kind of tension he describes between two quite different frames of reference, the commonsensical and rationalistic view of scientific scepticism on the one hand, and the primitive belief in the supernatural on the other, is quite precisely one of the things Dickens has suggested by dwelling on "the romantic side of familiar things," and played upon throughout the novel.

Freud's formulation that "an uncanny experience occurs

either when infantile complexes which have been repressed are once more revived by some impression, or when the primitive beliefs which have been surmounted seem once more to be confirmed" is incomplete insofar as it leaves out the tension created by two competing frames of reference, necessary to any uncanny experience, and suggests that any "return of the repressed" might be experienced as uncanny. This is not true, for what makes a particular instance of the return of the repressed an uncanny one is the fact that repressed material has to return in a particular way. An unconscious memory or fantasy is revived, but does not cease on that account to be repressed; if it did, the experience would simply be one of remembering. Rather, the memory or fantasy is revived subject to the conditions of a particular kind of distortion. But the distortion in this case does not work (as it would, for example, in the case of dreams or neurotic symptoms) so much upon the memory itself as, in a manner of speaking, upon the ego itself. Through some external chance, a repressed memory is revived more fully than we would normally allow, with the result that instead of rendering the details of that memory ambiguous (through the familiar forms of distortion), it is our very selves that seem to us ambiguous and strange. This is why, no doubt, Freud speaks of *déjà vu*, *déjà raconté* and *fausse reconnaissance* as the "positive counterparts" of feelings of depersonalization and derealization.[16]

These are difficult problems, and little understood by psychoanalytic (or any other) theory. Indeed, Freud said of precisely this area, only two years before his death, that it "is so obscure and has been so little mastered scientifically" that it is scarcely possible to write of it at all.[17] Perhaps the best way to elucidate the peculiar form in which repressed material returns in experiences of uncanniness is to draw an analogy with what Freud sees as the dynamics of wit, in which "a preconscious thought is given over for a moment to unconscious revision and the outcome of this is at once grasped by conscious perception." [18] In jokes of all kinds, as in experiences of uncanniness, something repressed is momentarily allowed into consciousness, relatively undisguised. Again, however, what is repressed does not on that account cease to be repressed; now, whatever defensive functions have been abdicated by the usual kinds of distortion to which repressed drives and memories are subject become shifted onto the field of the affects themselves. The analogy between jokes and the uncanny not only may help us to clarify the dynamics of the uncanny, but suggests further a connection between what I have been saying about the uncanny in *Bleak House* with what I noted as Dickens's primary technique of suspended animation in the opening number: the elaborate punning we saw there (not only lexical, but the punning of images, characters, and whole situations) makes use of exactly such semi-disguised repetitions as occur in the uncanny experience of *déjà vu*.

The quality of a double perspective, which is common both to the kind of wit Dickens makes use of in *Bleak House* and to the uncanny, we could say, is accounted for in psychoanalytic theory by a dramatic cooperation between the conscious, preconscious, and unconscious. This is, too, the most prominent feature of another class of psychological phenomena that have also been cited by psychoanalysts as uncanny, the hypnoid phenomena. [19] These embrace a fairly large number of experiences in addition to hypnosis proper. They include hypnagogic states (states between waking and sleeping), somnambulism, fugue states (states in which one is seemingly conscious, but of which, after a return to "normal," one has no memory), multiple personality, and the traumatic neuroses. And they are related to or involved in other kinds of pathology as well—in particular the aura of epileptic seizures and certain kinds of hysterical attacks. With the exception of hypnagogic states, all of these phenomena involve movements into altered states of consciousness followed by amnesias for these altered states (and, in the traumatic neuroses, amnesia for the events surrounding the trauma). And most (not excepting hypnagogic states) are transitional phenomena, both insofar as they involve transitions between states of consciousness and manifest features of sleeping and waking experience simultaneously and insofar as they are reversible and relatively short-lived.

Dickens's interest in these phenomena, like his related interest in dreams, was life-long and crops up regularly in both the work and in the life.[20] It is not remarkable that a novelist should fill a novel with the dreams of his characters, but it is remarkable that the dreams of Dickens's characters in *Bleak House* almost always seem more like trances than dreams; and it is remarkable, too, that so many characters in fact experience trances proper.

Everyone in *Bleak House* dreams, but more often than not they daydream, or simply fall, like the Lord Chancellor, Lady Dedlock, and even Esther's doll, into abstracted states. The most dramatic of these waking dreams occurs in Esther's smallpox delirium and her search with Bucket for her mother. What these abstracted states (frequently described by Dickens, but never more so than in *Bleak House*) generally signify is the real-

ization that one has been caught up in an unintelligible existence. Mr. Snagsby's waking dreams and sleeping dreams are
typical:

There is disquietude in Cook's Court, Cursitor Street.
Black suspicion hides in that peaceful region. The mass of
Cook's-Courtiers are in their usual state of mind, no better and
no worse; but, Mr. Snagsby is changed, and his little woman
knows it.

For, Tom-all-Alone's and Lincoln's Inn Fields persist in
harnessing themselves, a pair of ungovernable coursers, to the
chariot of Mr. Snagsby's imagination; and Mr. Bucket drives;
and the passengers are Jo and Mr. Tulkinghorn; and the complete equipage whirls through the Law Stationery business at
wild speed, all round the clock. Even in the little front kitchen
where the family meals are taken, it rattles away at a smoking
pace from the dinner-table, when Mr. Snagsby pauses in carving
the first slice of the leg of mutton baked with potatoes, and stares
at the kitchen wall.

Mr. Snagsby cannot make out what it is that he has had to
do with. Something is wrong, somewhere; but what something,
what may come of it, to whom, when, and from which un-
thought and unheard of quarter, is the puzzle of his life. His
remote impressions of the robes and coronets, the stars and gar-
ters, that sparkle through the surface-dust of Mr. Tulkinghorn's
chambers; his veneration for the mysteries presided over by that
best and closest of his customers, whom all the Inns of Court,
all Chancery Lane, and all the legal neighbourhood agree to
hold in awe; his remembrance of Detective Mr. Bucket with his
forefinger, and his confidential manner impossible to be evaded
or declined; persuade him that he is a party to some dangerous
secret, without knowing what it is. And it is the fearful peculiar-
ity of this condition that, at any hour of his daily life, at any
opening of the shop-door, at any pull of the bell, at any entrance
of a messenger, or any delivery of a letter, the secret may take air

and fire, explode, and blow up—Mr. Bucket only knows whom.

For which reason, whenever a man unknown comes into the shop (as many unknown men do), and says, "Is Mr. Snagsby in?" or words to that innocent effect, Mr. Snagsby's heart knocks hard at his guilty breast. He undergoes so much from such inquiries, that when they are made by boys he revenges himself by flipping at their ears over the counter, and asking the young dogs what they mean by it, and why can't they speak out at once? More impracticable men and boys persist in walking into Mr. Snagsby's sleep, and terrifying him with unaccountable questions; so that often, when the cock at the little dairy in Cursitor Street breaks out in his usual absurd way about the morning, Mr. Snagsby finds himself in a crisis of nightmare, with his little woman shaking him, and saying, "What's the matter with the man!" (25)

What is the matter with Mr. Snagsby is what is the matter with almost everyone else in the novel—he knows that something awful and mysterious has happened and that he is somehow implicated in that mystery, but that is all. The question again is one of causes and relations, and the mystery is that like Chancery itself it seems to expand endlessly until it encompasses all experience. It must expand, moreover, just because it is such a mystery and because there is no logical way to get hold of it, much less to contain it. Mr. Snagsby has all the clues; we might also say he has all the answers. But what he does not have is the question—he does not know what crime has been committed.

The confusion between waking and sleeping manifested in Mr. Snagsby is repeated in innumerable characters in the novel. Some of these instances of trance are relatively conventional (that is, figurative)—Mr. Krook's "abstraction" (5) or Guppy's "dazed state" after seeing Lady Dedlock's portrait (7) or "the spell under which he seemed to labour" during his proposal to Esther (9), or his "air of one who was either imperfectly awake, or walking in his sleep" when he first sees Esther after her disfigurement (38), for example. Instances of this kind are the most common in the novel and may be read as emanating, if sometimes apparently indirectly, from the central and greatest power in the novel, the almost totemic influence of Chancery, from whose psychic thralldom none quite manages to escape. As Miss Flite describes it to Esther in a passage we have already touched on,

> ". . . there's a dreadful attraction in the place. Hush! don't mention it to our diminutive friend [Charley] when she comes in. Or it may frighten her. With good reason. There's a cruel attraction in the place. You *can't* leave it. And you *must* expect."
>
> I tried to assure her that this was not so. She heard me patiently and smilingly, but was ready with her own answer.
>
> "Aye, aye, aye! You think so, because I am a little rambling. Ve-ry absurd, to be a little rambling, is it not? Ve-ry confusing, too. To the head. I find it so. But, my dear, I have been there many years, and I have noticed. It's the Mace and Seal upon the table."
>
> What could they do, did she think? I mildly asked her.
>
> "Draw," returned Miss Flite. "Draw people on, my dear. Draw peace out of them. Sense out of them. . . . I have felt them even drawing my rest away in the night. Cold and glittering devils!" (35)

It is the very persistence of what is here the literally magnetic "spell" of Chancery, as Miss Flite calls it (35), and all its subsidiary spells, that perhaps softens somewhat the effect on the reader of what would normally be most striking instances of hypnoid and related states, such as Guster's "fits," in which, like Macbeth, Dickens tells us, she "murders sleep"—the sleep of the Cook's Courtiers as well as her own (11)—or Mrs. Snagsby's "becoming cataleptic," so that she "has to be carried up the narrow staircase like a grand piano" (25) or Mlle. Hortense's vengeful rage, which renders her "cataleptic with determination" (42) or Mr. Krook's alcoholic stupors, which "are always more like a fit than a nap" (20) or Lady Dedlock's behavior immediately before Tulkinghorn's murder, which, in another allusion to *Macbeth*, reminds the debilitated cousin of "inconvenient woman—who *will* getoutofbedandbawthstablishment—Shakespeare" (48).

These examples represent but the extreme forms of an externally represented state that has been familiar to us from the opening number, with the Lord Chancellor "outwardly directing his contemplation to the lantern in the roof" (1), Lady Dedlock's sitting at her window "looking out in the early twilight from her boudoir at a keeper's lodge" (2), and Esther's doll sitting "propped up in a great arm-chair . . . staring at . . . nothing" (3). And similarly there are in the novel a number of characters whose influence over others seems almost hypnotic, characters who, appropriately enough, play the role of inquisitors. Miss Barbary, "whose darkened face," Esther tells us, "had such power over me that it stopped me in the midst of my vehemence" (2), and Mr. Kenge, who silently gazes at Esther (3), are the first such characters, but the best example, certainly, is Inspector Bucket, who gets his way with people through a kind of suggestion that borders on the hypnotic:

"Yes! and lookee here, Mr. Snagsby," resumes Bucket, taking him aside by the arm, tapping him familiarly on the breast, and speaking in a confidential tone. "You're a man of the world, you know, and a man of business, and a man of sense. That's what *you are.*"

"I am sure I am obliged to you for your good opinion," returns the stationer, with his cough of modesty, "but—"

"That's what *you* are, you know," says Bucket. "Now, it an't necessary to say to a man like you, engaged in your business, which is a business of trust and requires a person to be wide awake and have his senses about him and his head screwed on tight (I had an uncle in your business once)—it an't necessary to say to a man like you, that it's the best and wisest way to keep little matters like this quiet. Don't you see? Quiet!"

"Certainly, certainly," returns the other.

"I don't mind telling *you*," says Bucket, with an engaging appearance of frankness, "that as far as I can understand it, there seems to be a doubt whether this dead person [Nemo] wasn't entitled to a little property, and whether this female [Lady Dedlock] hasn't been up to some games respecting that property, don't you see?"

"O!" says Mr. Snagsby, but not appearing to see quite distinctly.

"Now what *you* want," pursues Bucket, again tapping Mr. Snagsby on the breast in a comfortable and soothing manner, "is, that every person should have their rights according to justice. That's what *you* want."

"To be sure," returns Mr. Snagsby with a nod.

"On account of which, and at the same time to oblige a—do you call it, in your business, customer or client? I forget how my uncle used to call it."

"Why, I generally say customer myself," replies Mr. Snagsby.

"You're right!" returns Mr. Bucket, shaking hands with him quite affectionately,—"on account of which, and at the same time to oblige a real good customer, you mean to go down with me, in confidence, to Tom-all-Alone's, and to keep the whole thing quiet ever afterwards and never to mention it to any one. That's about your intentions, if I understand you?"

"You are right, sir. You are right," says Mr. Snagsby. (22)

Bucket of course has other, clearly magical powers. His intuition is virtually telepathic ("In a moment of hesitation on the part of Mr. Snagsby, Bucket dips down to the bottom of his mind") and his little stick of office is as good as a magic wand ("Mr. Bucket, coming behind some undersized young man . . . almost without glancing at him touches him with his stick; upon which the young man, looking round, instantly evaporates" [22]). He seems indeed to be something more than man. To Mr. Snagsby he seems "to possess an unlimited number of eyes" (22) and to Jo (who "dustn't name him," a sure sign of his totemic significance) he appears to be "in all manner of places, all at wanst" (46). Such is his influence over Snagsby—and this clearly bespeaks a power allied to hypnosis—that after their first encounter, Mr. Snagsby "goes homeward so confused by the events of the evening, that he is doubtful of the reality of the streets through which he goes—doubtful of the reality of the moon that shines above him" (22).

In the end, however, none of the trancelike or uncanny experiences of the characters of *Bleak House* are so intensely drawn as Esther's. Not only is she the source of uncanny feelings in others, but she has had uncanny experiences of her own, beginning as early as her removal to the Misses Donnys' school at Reading, where the "unreal air of everything at Greenleaf" made her seem "almost to have dreamed rather than really lived my old life at my godmother's" (3). Esther's experiences of this kind become more intense as she moves closer to the discovery of her identity—for example, in the passages I have already quoted in which she sees her mother for the first time and then is surprised by her shortly after in the keeper's lodge. Esther's experiences are sufficiently intense and haunting to distinguish them, say, from Mr. Guppy's or Mr. George's experiences of *déjà vu*. They approach something like Mr. Snagsby's "crisis of nightmare" (25) and already we can see in them Esther becoming far more estranged from herself than is usual with her. Esther's regular tendency, indeed, is to view herself as it were from outside herself, a tendency which is chronically expressed by her talking to herself. (In parting from Richard and Ada after their marriage, she writes that "I should have been the worst of the three, if I had not severely said to myself, 'Now, Esther, if you do [break down], I'll never speak to you again!' " [52].) But her talking to herself is a willed and purposive trick of hers. In the "innumerable pictures" of herself that rush upon her in her meetings with Lady Dedlock, however, the split occurs far closer to the level of perception itself. [21]

Of course it is in Esther's smallpox crisis and the events immediately surrounding it that her experiences of this kind are most intense and bizarre. That crisis comes in the novel's tenth number, just at the novel's halfway point (always significant for Dickens), which Dickens had confided to Miss Coutts was to contain the novel's "great turning idea" and the writing of which had kept him, he said, "in a perpetual scald and boil." [22] We have already learned in the previous number that Esther is in fact Lady Dedlock's daughter, but Esther herself is still entirely ignorant of her identity when Charley announces that Jenny, the brickmaker's wife, has been caring for a young orphan boy from London, and Esther resolves to go and see what she can do:

THE UNCANNY

It was a cold, wild night, and the trees shuddered in the wind. The rain had been thick and heavy all day, and with little intermission for many days. None was falling just then, however. The sky had partly cleared, but was very gloomy—even above us, where a few stars were shining. In the north and north-west, where the sun had set three hours before, there was a pale dead light both beautiful and awful; and into it long sullen lines of cloud waved up, like a sea stricken immoveable as it was heaving. Towards London, a lurid glare overhung the whole dark waste; and the contrast between these two lights, and the fancy which the redder light engendered of an unearthly fire, gleaming on all the unseen buildings of the city, and on all the faces of its many thousands of wondering inhabitants, was as solemn as might be.

I had no thought, that night—none, I am quite sure—of what was soon to happen to me. But I have always remembered since, that when we had stopped at the garden-gate to look up at the sky, and when we went upon our way, I had for a moment an undefinable impression of myself as being something different from what I then was. I know it was then, and there, that I had it. I have ever since connected the feeling with that spot and time, and with everything associated with that spot and time, to the distant voices in the town, the barking of a dog, and the sound of wheels coming down the miry hill. (31)

This is an odd passage, to say the very least. It would be odd enough if it only described that sky which seems to have been split in half, a description which like the sky itself (or like the novel, which it might also be describing) is at once "beautiful and awful." Its function is clearly enough to anticipate the smallpox which is carried from Jo (the passage is immediately followed by Jo's first meeting with Esther) to Charley to Esther, and which finally takes Esther back to Chesney Wold, where she learns that she is Lady Dedlock's daughter. But Dickens goes out of his way (and beyond the conventions of such forebodings) to internalize the divided sky as a deep division in Esther's very sense of self: "I had for a moment an undefinable impression of myself as being something different from what I then was." Esther's words here, like her description of her twelfth birthday (3), are entirely enigmatic—that is, there is absolutely no way in which we can decipher what she means here. "Then" can refer only to that time, and not some previous time, so that she must be saying that she felt herself not simply to be changing or even changed, but literally not herself. Esther is careful however not to turn to that conventional and figurative phrase, and careful too not to tell us what she means by "something different." (Indeed, we cannot even be sure whether "something" is being used here as a noun or adverb.) Esther herself knows the experience is a curious and possibly supernatural one. Like Dickens, she is apparently interested in such experiences for their own sake, and she writes here as an amateur psychologist of sorts—in a voice she will adopt again in describing her delirium—being sure to emphasize that the feeling preceded her meeting with Jo, that she had not then thought of the possibility of contagion, and that she is certain of her memory by the precise association of the feeling with "that spot and time."

It is difficult to imagine such a passage written by one who has not experienced feelings of depersonalization as strong as Esther's, whereas in the descriptions of the trancelike states of others there is little that could not be founded on external observation. This is even more evident in Esther's description of the first stages of her illness:

THE UNCANNY

It was a great morning when I could tell Ada all this [that Charley would recover and that she would not be disfigured] as she stood out in the garden; and it was a great evening, when Charley and I at last took tea together in the next room. But, on that same evening, I felt that I was stricken cold.

Happily for both of us, it was not until Charley was safe in bed again and placidly asleep, that I began to think the contagion of her illness was upon me. I had been able easily to hide what I felt at tea-time, but I was past that already now, and I knew that I was rapidly following in Charley's steps.

I was well enough, however, to be up early in the morning, and to return my darling's cheerful blessing from the garden, and to talk with her as long as usual. But I was not free from an impression that I had been walking about the two rooms in the night, a little beside myself, though knowing where I was; and I felt confused at times—with a curious sense of fulness, as if I were becoming too large altogether. (31)

Esther falls ill with characteristic self-control. She is in fact ashamed of her illness, and, in one sense, rightly so. It is, as she calls it, a "secret" (31) that she confides at first only to Charley, who has become here the living reincarnation of Esther's doll, as well as the reincarnation of Esther herself as the child who read her own guilt in her godmother's face—for Charley is sure "It's my doing!" (31).[23] This does not mean, of course, that Esther has become Miss Barbary; but it does mean, inasmuch as the smallpox that has literally branded her can be traced back in several ways to the sexual and social crimes which gave birth to her (having originated either in Tom-all-Alone's, a property "in Chancery" and indeed connected with Jarndyce and Jarndyce [16], or in the "pestiferous and obscene" graveyard in which her father has been buried, "whence malignant diseases are communicated to the bodies of our dear brothers and sisters who have not departed" [11]),[24] that the guilt of Esther's birth has at last caught up with her and now threatens to overwhelm her. Esther again is "beside" herself. She virtually sleepwalks and is "confused at times—with a curious sense of fulness, as if I were becoming too large altogether." And both her sleepwalking and her assertion of "fulness" again suggest hypnoid states. Changes of size in one's body image in fact are a characteristic experience in the first stages of hypnosis.[25]

It is of course with the crisis of her smallpox fever and its accompanying delirium that Esther's self-estrangement becomes most dramatic:

> I lay ill through several weeks, and the usual tenor of my life became like an old remembrance. But this was not the effect of time, so much as of the change in all my habits, made by the helplessness and inaction of a sick room. Before I had been confined to it many days, everything else seemed to have retired into a remote distance, where there was little or no separation between the various stages of my life which had been really divided by years. In falling ill, I seemed to have crossed a dark lake, and to have left all my experiences, mingled together by the great distance, on the healthy shore. . . .
>
> While I was very ill, the way in which these divisions of time became confused with one another, distressed my mind exceedingly. At once a child, an elder girl, and the little woman I had been so happy as, I was not only oppressed by cares and difficulties adapted to each station, but by the great perplexity of endlessly trying to reconcile them. I suppose that few who have not been in such a condition can quite understand what I mean, or what painful unrest arose from this source.
>
> For the same reason I am almost afraid to hint at that time in my disorder—it seemed one long night, but I believe there

were both nights and days in it—when I laboured up colossal staircases, ever striving to reach the top, and ever turned, as I have seen a worm in a garden path, by some obstruction, and labouring again. I knew perfectly at intervals, and I think vaguely at most times, that I was in my bed; and I talked with Charley, and felt her touch, and knew her very well; yet I would find myself complaining "O more of these never-ending stairs, Charley—more and more—piled up to the sky, I think!" and labouring on again.

Dare I hint at that worse time when, strung together somewhere in great black space, there was a flaming necklace, or ring, or starry circle of some kind, of which *I* was one of the beads! And when my only prayer was to be taken off from the rest, and when it was such inexplicable agony and misery to be a part of the dreadful thing? (35)

This is not of course Dickens's first description of the delirium of fever. Oliver Twist falls into a long illness after his imprisonment at the police office in Mutton Hill, which "seemed [to him] to have been a long and troubled dream" (*Oliver Twist*, 12). Dick Swiveller's illness, in which he is nursed by the Marchioness (*The Old Curiosity Shop*, 64), perhaps the most famous of the troubled fevers in Dickens before *Bleak House*, is more fully described than Oliver's, but neither approaches the intensity or centrality of Esther's crisis. And Esther's crisis, moreover, continues long after the disease has left her, a point that is marked and underscored by her permanent disfigurement.

Recuperating at Chesney Wold, Esther meets Lady Dedlock and at last learns who she is. The effect of this revelation is to make Esther "as weak and helpless at first as I had ever been in my sick chamber" (36). Having discovered who she is, she is immediately horrified by the thought that others might find out too, so that she conceives, she says, "a terror of myself," knowing that she is a "witness" (the word is yet another of many in the novel that have both religious and legal reverberations) against her mother, and feeling the "visitation" of her parents' sins has at last come down on her, as Miss Barbary had prophesied. Half-distracted, she wanders one evening about the grounds of Chesney Wold, where she sees one lighted window in the darkness that might be her mother's—an image that is intended perhaps to recall the "flaming necklace" or "starry circle" of Esther's delirium, and further recalls an earlier view we have had of Chesney Wold, where "from distant openings in the trees, the row of windows in the long drawing-room, where my Lady's picture hangs over the great chimney-piece, is like a row of jewels set in a black frame" (12):

> The way was paved here, like the terrace overhead, and my footsteps from being noiseless made an echoing sound upon the flags. Stopping to look at nothing, but seeing all I did see as I went, I was passing quickly on, and in a few moments should have passed the lighted window, when my echoing footsteps brought it suddenly into my mind that there was a dreadful truth in the legend of the Ghost's Walk; that it was I, who was to bring calamity upon this stately house; and that my warning feet were haunting it even then. Seized with an augmented terror of myself which turned me cold, I ran from myself and everything, retraced the way by which I had come, and never paused until I had gained the lodge-gate, and the park lay sullen and black behind me. (36).

The division in Esther's consciousness which becomes so deep in her smallpox crisis and in the events surrounding it, the events having to do with her discovery of her identity, clearly derives from her illegitimacy and what she perceives as "the fault" with which she had been born, and which she says made her feel at the same time "guilty and yet innocent" (3). That "fault" creates two Esthers—indeed, perhaps, innumerable Esthers—for it is a fault of such magnitude and centrality that it necessarily robs her self of any coherence and robs any self she might assume of coherence.

Her story has to do with repairing the fault and unifying her self, and the centrality of her story in the novel lies in the fact that all its other stories are also about analogous faults—the faults of dislocation in love life, home life, and in the relations between parents and children. The number of celibate people in the novel (those who have been disappointed in love, the bachelors, spinsters, widows, and widowers) is awesome. The list includes John Jarndyce, Nemo, Ada, Miss Barbary, Lawrence Boythorn, Mr. Tulkinghorn, Miss Flite, Mr. Gridley, Mr. Guppy, Krook, Mr. George, Rosa's mother, Mlle. Hortense, Mr. Turveydrop, Phil Squod, Tony Jobling, Volumnia Dedlock, Mrs. Woodcourt, Mr. Vholes, and Mrs. Rouncewell. But those who are not celibate are for the most part no better off. One imagines that though Sir Leicester married Lady Dedlock "for love" (2), theirs is scarcely a passionate union, if it could be said to be a union at all; they have no children. And theirs is not the only barren marriage—the Snagsbys, the Badgers, and the Buckets are all childless. Most of the children who have managed to find their way into the world are, like Esther, hardly fortunate in their births. There are of course the orphans, Jo, Charley, Guster, Judy and Bart Smallweed, Richard, Ada, and (in effect, though not in fact) Esther herself.

THE UNCANNY

There are the crippled (Caddy's deaf and dumb child, for example) and the little monsters who are so fortunate as to have parents, the little Jellybys, Pardiggles, and Skimpoles. In fact, there are only three families of any prominence at all in the novel that are not in some way mutilated or deficient, and those are Mr. Rouncewell the Ironmaster's, Matthew Bagnet's, and of course finally Esther's and Allan's.

Esther does manage finally to repair the fault, for she both finds herself a husband and raises a family, although the price she pays, the literal replacement of her old face with a new one, is enormously heavy. And although Esther underplays the change, we should not on that account forget how dramatic the change has been. Here is Esther's own description of her first look at her new face:

> My hair had not been cut off, though it had been in danger more than once. . . . I let it down, and shook it out, and went up to the glass upon the dressing-table. There was a little muslin curtain drawn across it. I drew it back: and stood for a moment looking through such a veil of my own hair, that I could see nothing else. Then I put my hair aside, and looked at the reflection in the mirror; encouraged by seeing how placidly it looked at me. I was very much changed—O very, very much. At first, my face was so strange to me, that I think I should have put my hands before it and started back, but for the encouragement I have mentioned [of counting her blessings and returning to "the childish prayer" of her twelfth birthday]. Very soon it became more familiar, and then I knew the extent of the alteration in it better than I had done at first. It was not like what I had expected; but I had expected nothing definite, and I dare say anything definite would have surprised me.
>
> I had never been a beauty, and had never thought myself one; but I had been very different from this. It was all gone now. (36)

THE UNCANNY

Somewhat paradoxically, it is only when Esther's fault is externalized here as a new and in itself faulty face—in what is surely one of the grimmest instances in the novel of the revelation of "the romantic side of familiar things"—that her self-division begins to be repaired; but then scar tissue is, after all, more properly a sign of healing than of disease.

If the price Esther pays is great, then we must also say that the resolution of her divided selves is far from complete. She may not at the end of the novel still feel "guilty and yet innocent" and she surely has established a strong and whole identity for herself, but a number of things at the close of the novel also suggest irresolution, and that the paradox of "the romantic side of familiar things," the paradox of double perspective, and the paradox of the uncanny have not been entirely overcome. Most important of these is the novel's curious last sentence—or fragment of a sentence, rather—which ends with Esther, still thinking of her lost beauty, asking—or beginning to ask, rather—a question: "even supposing——" (67). "Supposing" what? "Supposing" it had all happened differently? The question, in its very vagueness, takes us right back to the beginning of the novel. And another curious detail takes us backward rather than forward: Esther and Allan come to live in a house that is a virtual copy, or double, of Bleak House.' The implications of this duplication are intensely complicated, bound up as they are with the elaborate ruse John Jarndyce comes up with to hand over Esther to Allan and so save her from her planned marriage to her guardian—a marriage that, for all the affection between Esther and Jarndyce, nevertheless would have represented but another of the numerous dislocated and crippled marriages in the novel, for it is clear that it would have been a marriage without sex and without children. Even at that point in the novel where Esther ought we feel to be allowed one unambiguous movement forward, and one movement of unambiguous freedom from a past that has almost killed her, the shadow of that past falls upon her, and we discover ourselves still caught up in the uncanny pattern of circularity. Love may be homesickness after all.[26]

IV

The crucial factor in Freud's formulations of uncanny experience is repression: it is the fact of something "forgotten" that creates a division within us and allows an uncanny experience to occur, for without a forgetting there is no ground for the tension between the two competing frames of reference or double perspective that characterizes uncanny experience. Without such a "forgetting" the familiar never can become strange or romantic to us. In *Bleak House*, Dickens has made use of a number of forgotten things—for example, the common fantasy expressed in fairy tales and romances that we are not our parents' children but secretly the children of kings and queens. Indeed, we can say that Dickens has made use of the whole complex of forgotten fantasies and wishes that Freud calls "the family romance." But he has also created his own forgotten things, such as the clues we have seen him dropping in the opening number, whose significance is apparent to us only long after they have been first introduced to us. And of course he has created, too, an atmosphere of forgetting. At the very beginning of the novel we are introduced to Jarndyce and Jarndyce as a thing forgotten—even as it is with us—for the "suit has, in course of time, become so complicated, that no man alive knows what it means" (1), and Esther is specifically commanded by her godmother to "Forget your mother" (3)—even though she has never known a mother she could forget.

It is such things forgotten that place us in what I have described as a state of continual circularity or peripety as well as enforce the division of self in Esther and a host of other kinds of division, including the most prominent example of division in the novel, that of the double narrative. While the novel's two narratives are opposites in many ways (the one being masculine, aggressive, and angry, and interested only in the present, the other being feminine, retiring, self-involved, and reflecting only on what is already past), it is nevertheless sometimes difficult to tell them apart. Esther, in particular, often falls into the voice of the other narrator,[27] and this suggests that we may read them as alter egos. (This is of course actually true, inasmuch as both are alter egos of Dickens, but it is also imaginatively true if we read the other narrator as Esther's persona—and in fact the only way to explain the double narrative according to even the loosest standards of "realism" is to say that Esther has chosen to write in the first person, but has written an "other," third-person narrative to cover those events of her story in which she has not directly participated.)

Dickens is famous for his use of alter egos, doubles, or what Taylor Stoehr calls "surrogates." [28] *Bleak House* has no pair of doubles so spectacular as Dickens's most famous pair, Sidney Carton and Charles Darnay, just as *Bleak House* does not explore the phenomenon of divided consciousness as explicitly as *The Mystery of Edwin Drood* evidently was to have done.[29] Nevertheless, the novel has more than its share of alter egos. There are a large number of minor pairs of alter egos made up of characters who serve analogous functions either in the plot or in the thematic structure and who usually have a number of traits in common. Mrs. Bagnet, for example, is paired with Inspector Bucket in more things than the similarity between their names. Both are figures of magical power, intelligence, and goodness, and both have their magical props: Bucket has his little staff of office which can make people instantly evaporate (21) and Mrs. Bagnet has her umbrella which she generally uses "as a wand" or "to arrest the attention of tradesmen" (24). More importantly, both Mr. Bucket and Mrs. Bagnet are involved in missions of mercy involving long journeys. Mrs. Bagnet takes off for Chesney Wold at an instant's notice to reclaim George Rouncewell's mother just as Bucket chases up and down the country after Esther's mother.

But such pairs of alter egos in Dickens almost invariably have their crucial differences as well. Like Carton and Darnay, they always contain profound oppositions, and so instead of being simple duplicates, they are duplicates with variations. In fact, they represent in terms of characters the sort of circular pattern I have already examined in terms of narrative in my last chapter. Thus Mrs. Bagnet is surrounded by a large family while Bucket is in contrast pointedly childless—indeed, Bucket makes the point to the Bagnets (49). Opposition may be more apparent than similarity as in the case, for example, of David Copperfield and Uriah Heep, and this is true in *Bleak House*'s most important sets of doubles, those formed out of the triad of Esther, Lady Dedlock, and Mlle. Hortense, all of whom strikingly resemble one another physically and are of course confused with one another at various points in the novel, but otherwise seem to have nothing in common—except, of course, in the case of Esther and Lady Dedlock, a biological bond. What they have most in common, we might say, are opposite personalities. Lady Dedlock and Mlle. Hortense together suggest the extreme poles of the opposition between inhibition and passion. Lady Dedlock (like another of her doubles, Miss Barbary) is characterized by her "freezing mood" (2), while Mlle. Hortense is characterized by passion that stops not even at murder, and her passion represents all that Lady Dedlock has suppressed.

It is only by apprehending the doubleness of Lady Dedlock and Mlle. Hortense, moreover, that we can apprehend the central importance of the murder of Tulkinghorn. Mlle. Hortense is obviously a minor character, and her motives for the killing apparently have to do with her wounded pride and sense that she has "established a claim upon Mr. Tulkinghorn" (54) which he has not honored—they apparently have no connection, in other words, with the novel's chief plots or thematic interests. But the apparent fortuitousness of Tulkinghorn's murder is only apparent. We as readers are apt to feel that the murder accomplishes several things, the chief of which is to strike a blow for both Lady Dedlock and Esther, to both of whom Tulkinghorn represents the powerful ascendancy of their guilty secret, while the murder secondarily represents a blow against the institution that Mr. Tulkinghorn has come to personify, the Court of Chancery. We as readers, that is to say, cannot easily separate Mlle. Hortense's motives from our own. And this is true of Lady Dedlock and Esther as well, both of whom significantly feel a certain guilty horror at the murder (52 and 55), while Mlle. Hortense is absolutely without remorse. It is as though Dickens had simply displaced the guilt for the murder onto Lady Dedlock and Esther. Lady Dedlock, to be sure, herself becomes at once a suspect, and the murder triggers her "flight" (55)—which itself suggests that she has another double in the novel. Indeed, the plot almost treats her as guilty, and it is curiously the arrest of Mlle. Hortense that is apt to seem to us fortuitous, while Bucket's hunting of Lady Dedlock and her death at the gates to her husband's burying ground seem more appropriate to the fate of a murderess.

Esther occupies an intermediate position between the extreme poles of Mlle. Hortense's passionate impulsiveness and Lady Dedlock's "freezing mood." She occupies, in other words, the position of conflict and ambivalence that is the more usual human lot. In most important ways, her connections with Mlle. Hortense and Lady Dedlock are by virtue of opposition, and yet there are similarities beyond the physical resemblances. In a very strange scene, Mlle. Hortense offers Esther her services as maid, *gratis* (23). There seems to be no purpose in this scene except to establish Mlle. Hortense in analogous relationships with Esther and Lady Dedlock: toward both she becomes a rejected suitor. And this establishes a further connection with Esther, who has been rejected by Miss Barbary and in some sense by Lady Dedlock as well. Thus all three women do seem to us oddly connected, as if each represented hidden sides of the others.

One of the points of such doublings of characters, of course, and it is a characteristic point in Dickens, is to realize the possibilities of alternate lives and alternate ways of living. Miss Flite and Mr. Gridley, another of the novel's pairs of alter egos, show us two ways of dealing with Chancery. Mrs. Jellyby and Mrs. Pardiggle show us two ways of reconciling (or failing to reconcile) philanthropic careers with home life. Mr. and

Mrs. Snagsby show us two ways of coping with a mystery, and so on. Esther connects with all of these pairs, and, as in the Mlle. Hortense–Lady Dedlock pair, she again occupies an intermediate and uncomfortably conflicted position between extremes. Described in this way, however, *Bleak House* sounds like a commonsensical if somewhat mechanical exercise in Aristotelian ethics, and yet "commonsensical" and "mechanical" are about the last words we would use to describe the peculiar atmosphere of the novel. For Dickens has repeatedly undercut the commonsensicality of his lesson by virtue of the very intensity of his empathy with the extremes: Esther's progress shows us her arriving at the mean as much by embracing extremes (in imagination if not in deed) as by avoiding them, and this is even more the case for the reader. The world of *Bleak House* is one that we view through *both* Mr. and Mrs. Snagsby's eyes: it is a world that alternately appears to make no sense at all and to make all too coherent, indeed positively paranoid, sense—a world in which alternately nothing seems to be connected and everything seems to be connected. It is an uncanny world, in short, in which everything is constantly in movement between the poles of the familiar and the romantic.

This suggests a further point, or effect, at least, of the doublings of character. Just as Dickens has by dwelling "on the romantic side of familiar things" rendered causal relations problematic, so too has he rendered the notion of identity problematic. Esther's crisis, of course, is of the sort we nowadays call a crisis of identity, and we have seen that it is resolved in no simple or unambiguous way (compare it, for example, with the end of Oliver Twist's quest for identity). But it is not simply her identity that is problematic in the novel: it is almost everyone's, for almost everyone at some point is either put in the position of the twelve-year-old Esther who is searching to know what she has done and what secret haunts her or is put in the position of Lady Dedlock, and suffers from some dislocation between past and present identities. In this sense, the multiple and divided selves of the novel are not simply the products of Dicken's pyrotechnic toying with uncanny effects, but the necessary effect of living in a world which is chiefly characterized by its repression and suppression of the past. And in Dickens, as in Freud, the repressed returns, and returns, and returns.

CHAPTER FOUR

A BIOGRAPHICAL EXCURSION

*"What could you expect
from such an uncanny genius?"*
—Kate (Dickens) Perugini

I

MOST people know at least some of the stories of Dickens's life. Just about everyone who has read a Dickens novel at school, for example, knows how Dickens worked as a child in some sort of hideous factory while his father was imprisoned for debt. There are good reasons, moreover, why the greatest storyteller of the nineteenth century should himself have become the subject of great stories, and Dickens's own tendencies to self-dramatization and self-melodramatization are not the least of these. His letters are filled with mock-heroic accounts of his activities, and in the novels he of course makes free use of his own life—the several pages he lifts, virtually without alteration, for David Copperfield's account of his life at Murdstone and Grinby's (and indeed much of his boyhood) from the autobiographical fragment he had written a few years before are but the most famous examples of this. The point here, however, is not so much that the life appears in the works, or that the life can be regarded as a source for the works, as that the life as we have it *is* one of the works. [1]

The really astonishing thing, to my mind, about Dickens's life is how much of it finds its way into the work unmediated. Of course every writer can write only out of his own experience (insofar as he can imagine only through his own experience), and thus in theory—if only we knew enough—we should be able to identify "sources" for every element in any text. In practice, however, our knowledge is so incomplete, and those sources are so complexly transformed by the creative imagination as to be untraceable—often even by the writer himself. Not so with Dickens. In *Bleak House*, in fact, it is difficult to find things for which we *cannot* identify sources. We have already touched very briefly on the work of John Butt and Kathleen Tillotson, who in their chapter on "The Topicality of *Bleak House*" in *Dickens at Work* (London: Methuen, 1957) have amply demonstrated the extent to which Chancery reform, sanitary reform, Exeter Hall philanthropy (*à la* Mrs. Jellyby), Puseyism (*à la* Mrs. Pardiggle), the newly formed Detective branch of the Metropolitan Police (of which Inspector Bucket is the first member to appear in English fiction), and even the difficulties of keeping house for a soldier (*à la* Mrs. Bagnet) were all subjects Dickens had culled from the newspapers and all subjects "in the public mind." [2] Nor is their list anything like complete. Mlle. Hortense was recognized by contemporaries as based upon a Belgian-born murderess, Maria Manning, whose arrogance and contempt for her prosecutors in the courtroom had been a sensation. [3] Parallels were drawn between Lady Dedlock's flight and a famous scandal of the day.[4] Jo's ordeal before the coroner's inquest at the Sol's Arms is taken virtually verbatim from the examination of another crossing-sweeper whose testimony had been printed in Dickens's own *Household Narrative of Current Events* the year before he began work on *Bleak House*.[5] And the list goes on and on. Lawrence Boythorn and Harold Skimpole were recognized as portraits of Walter Savage Landor and Leigh Hunt, respectively.[6] Guster, the Snagsby's young servant girl, is the product of a baby farm at Tooting which had been in 1849 rather more notorious—and deadly— than, say, New York's Willowbrook State School for the Mentally Retarded is today.[7] And so on.

Now this, it should be remembered, is simply a list—and incomplete at that—of sources that can be identified today by going back to newspapers of the period. It is a list of sources that would have already been familiar at least to newspaper-reading readers of the novel—and that fact suggests of course an additional meaning in "the romantic side of familiar things." But we can also draw up equally long lists of sources of other sorts. There are the topographical sources which would have been familiar at least to Londoners. Tulkinghorn's chambers, the Sol's Arms, Coavinses sponging house, and Nemo's burying-ground have all been identified, but of course all of the London neighborhoods in *Bleak House* (and in all of Dickens) are drawn from life.[8] Londoners, however, would not have recognized the name Tom-all-Alone's—nor its locale, which remains curiously and uncharacteristically vague—but residents of the Chatham of thirty years before might have recalled Tom-all-Alone's as the name of a recluse's hut built upon a piece of waste ground near the town; and if they remembered that it had been used during

Dickens's boyhood there as a site for war games, they might have understood the private joke in Dickens's description of Tom-all-Alone's as a place where ruined houses fall with "a crash and a cloud of dust, like the springing of a mine" (16).[9] Similarly, residents of Manchester might have recognized the appropriateness of Dickens's naming his young physician to the poor after Allan's Court, one of the worst streets of one of the worst slums of their city (in which sanitary conditions were so bad that the whole street had to be evacuated during the cholera epidemic of 1832), though of course in Allan Woodcourt's name Dickens is also announcing Allan's intentions toward Esther.[10]

We have not really even begun to look at Dickens's private sources for *Bleak House,* and yet I hope my readers will already have begun to feel that there may be some truth in my claim that it is difficult to find elements in the novel for which we cannot find originals. When I first decided to study *Bleak House* in detail, the very first task I assigned myself was to delve into the blue books on Chancery. I began with the report of a Chancery Commission completed in 1826, just the year before Dickens himself entered the legal world as an office boy for Ellis and Blackmore.[11] When I opened this hefty and musty folio quite at random, my eye fell upon the name of one Mr. Joseph Blower, a Chancery solicitor under examination by the Commission. Now this name rang a bell, a very tiny bell, to be sure, but a bell nonetheless. And I did not have to go far to find it— only as far as the third page of the novel in my copy, in fact, where we are introduced, for the first and last time, to "Mr. Blowers the eminent silk gown." This, I thought, is surely coincidental. Mr. Blowers's name is a self-explanatory comic invention on Dickens's part, and that's that. But that was not entirely that. I began to read Mr. Blower's testimony and as soon as I learned its subject, another bell, rather larger than the first, was sounded: for Mr. Blower happened to be testifying this day about a then particularly important Chancery suit, the case of Stevens vs. Guppy.[12] I closed up my volume and stared off into space, I believe, for some minutes—grateful that Stevens had not found his way into *Bleak House*. I know I never opened the *Report* of 1826 again.

II

Researching the way Dickens puts together his novels is rather like opening one of Mrs. Jellyby's closets—such wonderful and unexpected things keep tumbling out. But there is, in addition, something positively spooky about it, as in my experience with Messrs. Blower and Guppy. For one thing, it is much too easy. It is spooky too in the way that reading *Bleak House* is spooky: one encounters the same sort of insistent and ferocious, even if quite delicately veiled, resonances and reverberations between the life and the book that we have seen operating in the book itself and that, to my mind, are essential to the experience of reading the book. (Such resonances are of course a self-conscious subject of the book too—as when Dickens invokes the magical metaphor of London as "a vast glass, vibrating" [48].) This spooky reverberation is something we encounter not only in the kinds of small particular details I have been for the most part discussing, but in larger thematic concerns that recur in both the life and the work. And we can best see this by looking at some of Dickens's activities at the time he was conceiving and writing *Bleak House*.

"Activities" is rather an understatement. The Victorians,

we know, were rather an industrious lot, and Dickens was among the most active of Victorians. But he was never busier than when planning and writing *Bleak House*. He had founded his periodical *Household Words* at the end of 1849 and beginning of 1850—when finishing up *Copperfield*—and was working on it at full steam when, toward the end of February 1851—not, as Edgar Johnson says, in August—he confided to a friend that "the first shadows of a new story" were "hovering in a ghostly way" about him.[13] In the very months when he was winding up *Copperfield*, Dickens wrote almost forty articles for *Household Words*, and contributed an equal number in the months before he began to write *Bleak House*. During the same period his collaborators on other articles substantial enough to be included by Harry Stone in his *The Uncollected Writings of Charles Dickens: Household Words 1850–59* (Bloomington: Indiana University Press, 1968) number twenty-eight—the whole, in fact, of Stone's first volume. But of course Dickens's pen was everywhere in *Household Words*—just as his name was the only one to appear in its pages (indeed, on every one of its leaves). It was estimated by one of the *Household Words* staff writers that in 1854, when Dickens was beginning to relax both his control over the periodical and the energies he had been putting into writing for it, he "read nine hundred unsolicited contributions and used eleven after entirely rewriting them."[14] His corrections and revisions of even solicited pieces and those by the staff writers themselves were so extensive, moreover, that they often constituted rewriting.[15]

And this was scarcely all Dickens had to occupy him. His association with the immensely wealthy heiress, Angela Burdett-Coutts, fostered by their mutual interest in social reform, had by the late forties grown into a semi-formal partnership—with Miss Coutts supplying the money and Dickens the managerial talents to carry out a number of philanthropic schemes. Foremost among these was Urania Cottage, the "Home for Homeless Women" founded by Miss Coutts in then suburban Shepherd's Bush, and described by Dickens in *Household Words*. [16] This was a home designed to rehabilitate a small number of carefully screened prostitutes, with an eye to preparing them for eventual emigration. Though the original idea seems to have been Miss Coutts's, Dickens was responsible for planning and generally superintending all the business of the home down to the smallest detail. He found the cottage, leased it, renamed it, redecorated it, formulated its regulations, hired its matrons, recruited and examined its applicants, regularly visited it (often more than once a week) to oversee its operation and make important decisions, thought nothing of making emergency visits (usually to dismiss rebellious girls, of whom there were not a few) and meticulously reported on all his doings in his frequent letters to Miss Coutts. As with the editing of *Household Words*, Dickens's thoroughness was incredible, and can be appreciated only by reading through the Coutts letters. The following example, chosen at random, is typical:

> The blind-maker and I held a great council yesterday. And the blind-maker shewed me such good reasons for the common outside Venetian blinds, drawing up into cases, being at once the most enduring, the neatest, and cheapest, for our purpose, that I unhesitatingly concluded to order that kind. They will be done in about nine days. [17]

Only in 1856, nine years after the home was opened, did Dickens feel confident enough about the smoothness of its operation and pressured enough by his other duties to entrust at least some of the work he had done for Miss Coutts to his subeditor at *Household Words*, W. H. Wills, who in that year became her private secretary at an annual salary of £200. And again, Urania Cottage was only the chief of numerous projects in which Dickens aided Miss Coutts. Another scheme, which took up a good deal of Dickens's time while he was writing the opening of *Bleak House*, involved clearing slums and building in their place model dwellings for the poor, and the letters are filled with countless other projects, many of which required Dickens to investigate the cases of individuals who had applied to Miss Coutts for relief. [18]

But even this was not enough. As *David Copperfield* was drawing to a close, Dickens looked forward to returning to one of his oldest loves, amateur theatricals. [19] Plans were drawn up in the summer of 1850 for a three-night run of *Every Man in his Humour*, to be performed at Bulwer-Lytton's country estate at Knebworth, and as soon as *Copperfield* was finished in the fall, rehearsals began. As usual, Dickens assumed the choicest part (in this case, Bobadil), and both the greatest and smallest responsibilities of producer and stage manager. Out of these performances grew grander plans for a whole round of plays to be produced in London in the following spring. These were to be benefit performances for the Guild of Literature and Art, which Dickens and Bulwer-Lytton had, at Knebworth, just decided to found, in aid of unfortunate writers of established reputation as well as young but promising and needy ones. It was to his "Companions in the Guild of Literature and Art" that *Bleak House* was dedicated, and chief among the Guild's projects was a plan to build a series of small cottages which would be let free to indigent artists. While the Guild was being planned, there were more theatricals at Rockingham Castle in Northamptonshire, the home of Dickens's friends the Watsons (and, incidentally, the original of Chesney Wold). In the same month, January 1851, the first instalments of A *Child's History of England* appeared in *Household Words*, and in March the rehearsals for the Guild performances began. The troupe opened at Devonshire House, the Duke of Devonshire's London home, with Bulwer Lytton's *Not So Bad as We Seem* in May, to an audience that included the Queen. These performances continued in London at the Hanover Square Rooms until the beginning of August; and in November, the month in which the actual writing of *Bleak House* began, the company made the first of a series of provincial tours, which continued on and off until the following September. Excusing himself from an engagement with George Beadnell (the father of Maria, Dickens's first love), Dickens writes a typical account of what these theatrical activities involved. It is only slightly exaggerated.

> I am on stage all day, rehearsing with everybody, from breakfast until dinner. I preside at all the meals of the amateur company, and carve all the large joints. We carry into the country a perfect army of carpenters, gasmen, tailors, barbers, property-men, dressers and servants; all of whom have become accustomed to do everything with the utmost precision and accuracy under the Managerial eye, but none of whom would do anything right, if that luminary were withdrawn from any one of them for five minutes at a stretch. So I am perpetually hovering among and fluttering these small birds; at the last minute when the Hall has been filled for weeks, all sorts of impossible people want all sorts of impossible places; and have to be given the most urbane explanations. I then settle down for an hour or so before

the rising of the Curtain, to dress, enter upon two parts, something longer (I should say) than the whole play of Hamlet—am dressed fourteen times in the course of the night—and go to bed a little tired.[20]

There were other cares as well. At the end of 1847, Dickens learned that he would have to relinquish in four years his lease on Devonshire Terrace, in which he had lived since 1839. And even though he recognized the need for a larger house—seven of his children had been born in Devonshire Terrace—he had grown so fond of it that he put off serious house-hunting until the spring of 1851.[21] In July he settled, not altogether enthusiastically, on Tavistock House, Tavistock Square, on which he purchased a forty-five-year lease.[22] A decision to make extensive alterations in the house, however, created major problems and delayed the family's moving in (as well as the writing of *Bleak House*) until November. Dickens's letters of the time are filled with his anxieties about the house. He writes to his brother-in-law, Henry Austin:

I am perpetually wandering (in fancy) up and down the house and tumbling over workmen. When I feel that they are gone to dinner I become low. When I look forward to their total abstinence on Sunday, I become wretched. The gravy at dinner has a taste of glue in it. I smell paint in the sea. Phantom lime attends me all day long. I dream that I am a carpenter and can't partition off the hall.[23]

Now the first point of this review of Dickens's activities in 1850 and 1851 is that throughout Dickens's work on *Household Words*, his work at Miss Coutts's Home for Homeless Women and their plans to build model dwellings for the poor, his work on the amateur theatricals at Devonshire House, his work on the Guild of Literature and Art's projected cottages for needy artists, and his work on moving from Devonshire Terrace into Tavistock House, we can hardly fail to see a common theme or concern, and a theme, moreover, that we have already seen is central in *Bleak House:* I mean the concern we have seen registered in its title, the concern with houses, homeyness, and houselessness. It is no wonder Dickens dreamt he was a carpenter, and it is no wonder that, dreaming he was a particularly frustrated carpenter who couldn't "partition off the hall," we should find among the titles he was considering for his new novel "Tom-all-alone's. The Ruined house," "Tom-all-alone's. The Solitary house where The Wind howled," and "Bleak House and the East Wind." [24]

I should emphasize again that of course I do not mean to say that we can find an explanation for Dickens's fascination with houses in *Bleak House* in the large number of activities he was engaged in at the time that had to do with houses and household things. On the contrary, we might just as well look for the explanation for Dickens's fascination with houses in the life by referring back to the work.

The pattern here, in fact, is one that appears regularly in the work, and from very early on. For as early as *Pickwick Papers*, the concern with the condition of being housed, ill-housed, or houseless crops up with astonishing regularity. There, in Dickens's first novel, it of course creates the occasion for numerous comic and sentimental incidents, and is reflected too, perhaps, in the picaresque and peripatetic structure of the book. But it also figures importantly in the darker side of the novel, in most of the interpolated tales, that is, and in

BIOGRAPHICAL EXCURSION

Mr. Pickwick's incarceration in the Fleet. It is, however, with *Oliver Twist*, the next novel, that Dickens's concern with houses and houselessness reaches characteristic intensity and sharpness of focus. Just how intense and sharply focused the concern is here would require a much more elaborate demonstration than we have space for; but every reader of the novel must remember the obvious examples: Oliver's escape from the workhouse and from Sowerberry's, his walk to London, the home he finds at Fagin's, the home he finds at Mr. Brownlow's, his recapture by Sikes and return to Fagin's, the burglary at the Maylies' house in Chertsey. The concern continues with *Nicholas Nickleby* and Nicholas's and Kate's difficulties in finding homes for themselves and approaches again something of the intensity of *Oliver Twist* with *The Old Curiosity Shop* and *Barnaby Rudge*. In the former, it is of course Nell's and her grandfather's eviction from the shop and their subsequent travels that spring the novel's central events. In the latter, we have again the motif of a parent (or grandparent) fleeing a house with his (or her) child in Mrs. Rudge's flight from her cottage with Barnaby and of course also the ferocious destruction of numerous houses (and jails) in the Gordon Riots. In *Martin Chuzzlewit* there is the central episode of young Martin's exile in America, but there is too the fact that he has been in training as an architect. And so it goes, on beyond *Bleak House* to the collapse of the Clennam house in *Little Dorrit* and right on into *The Mystery of Edwin Drood*. And the significance of this lifelong concern of Dickens's remains much the same in all the works. As in *Bleak House*, where, as we have seen, it is especially intense, the condition of being housed or not generally represents whether one knows who one is or not, and that in turn is dependent most often either on one's relationship with one's parents or, equally important, on their relationship with the world and with their own past. In addition to being, like Oliver, orphaned, having, like Barnaby Rudge, for example, a guilty parent is as sure a way of finding oneself houseless (and, in Dickens, the most common way) as, to take examples from the same novel, having, like Hugh, a parent who fails to recognize the relationship, or, like Joe Willet, having a parent who fails to recognize that one is growing up, or, like Edward Chester, having a parent who simply doesn't like the way one is growing up.

The connection between houses and parents is natural enough, but of course there are also in the world grownups who find themselves without houses. And there are such grownups in Dickens too: Mrs. Rudge (and Barnaby Senior) and Grandfather Trent, for example, or, to come back to *Bleak House*, Lady Dedlock and Captain Hawdon. But still it is for their crimes *as parents* that they are punished with houselessness. Their stories remain subservient to the stories of their children (or grandchildren) and their houselessness always exists for us in relation to their children.

III

But there is yet more to learn from Dickens's activities. At the end of March, 1851, just at the time when Dickens's new story was beginning to shape itself in his mind, and at the very height of his activity in the amateur theatricals at Devonshire House, Dickens's father died. Dickens's wife, Kate, had herself been taken ill early in the same month, with what were probably hysterical attacks and had been sent to recuperate at Great Malvern;

Dickens had therefore been dividing his time—commuting, really—between there and London, almost a hundred miles away. Toward the end of the month he received word that his father was desperately ill from an old urinary complaint which he had neglected to have treated since his days in the Marshalsea—probably bladder stones.[25] Now Dickens wrote to his wife from London that his father

> was in that state from active disease (of the bladder) which he had mentioned to nobody, that mortification and delirium, terminating in speedy death, seemed unavoidable. Mr. Wade was called in, who instantly performed (without chloroform) the most terrible operation known in surgery, as the only chance of saving him. He bore it with astonishing fortitude, and I saw him directly afterwards—his room, a slaughter house of blood.[26]

He slept well that night and was the following morning, in Dickens's words, "as well . . . as anyone in such a state, so cut and slashed, can be." [27] But five days later, on the 31st of March, he was dead.[28]

Edgar Johnson is the only one of Dickens's biographers who records John Dickens's death in any detail, largely because Dickens himself evidently only spoke of it in any detail in his letters to his wife, many of which were not published until Walter Dexter collected them in 1935. And it is also perhaps because of Dickens's relative silence on the matter that scholars and critics have generally overlooked the fact that John Dickens's death coincides with a pivotal moment in his son's career—the inauguration of the "Dark Period." [29] These omissions on the part of both Dickens and his biographers are especially curious given the notorious importance of John Dickens in his son's early life and throughout the works.

In spite of Dickens's relative silence, we do have evidence of a profound upset in his life at the time of his father's death, for we know that during his father's last illness Dickens had an attack of insomnia that lasted for a week.[30] This he dealt with characteristically by pacing the London streets until dawn. Such "Night Walks," as he called them, were by no means new to him, but this particular series lasted for an unusual length of time, and out of it grew two articles for *Household Words* that are of especial relevance to *Bleak House* as containing Dickens's first writings about detectives and his first treatment of the original of Inspector Bucket, "The Metropolitan Protectives" and "On Duty with Inspector Field." [31] It is also this series of walks, most probably, that Dickens is referring to in his article "Night Walks," written ten years later for *All the Year Round*. It begins:

Some years ago, a temporary inability to sleep, referable to a distressing impression, caused me to walk about the streets all night, for a series of several nights. The disorder might have taken a long time to conquer, if it had been faintly experimented on in bed; but, it was soon defeated by the brisk treatment of getting up directly after lying down, and going out, and coming home tired at sunrise.

In the course of those nights, I finished my education in a fair amateur experience of houselessness. My principal object being to get through the night, my pursuit of it brought me into sympathetic relations with people who have no other object every night in the year.

The month was March, and the weather damp, cloudy, and cold. The sun not rising before half-past five, the night perspective looked sufficiently long at half-past twelve: which was about my time for confronting it. [32]

What is perhaps most striking in this passage about how Dickens dealt with the "distressing impression" left upon him by his father's death is that it shows us how directly that loss leads in his mind to "houselessness." That word becomes the keynote of the essay, and later in "Night Walks" Dickens will, indeed, begin to refer to himself in the third person as "Houselessness." But there is a good deal in "Night Walks" of interest to readers of *Bleak House* in addition to what it has to tell us about the relation between houselessness and the loss of parents, and that has to do with another aspect of Dickens's particular manner of coping with his own upset. Later in the essay, after touring several of London's jails—always a topic associated for him with his father, Dickens tells us:

> I chose next to wander by Bethlehem Hospital; partly, because it lay on my road round Westminster; partly, because I had a night fancy in my head which could be best pursued within sight of its walls and dome. And the fancy was this: Are not the sane and the insane equal at night as the sane lie a dreaming? Are not all of us outside this hospital, who dream, more or less in the condition of those inside it, every night of our lives? Are we not nightly persuaded, as they daily are, that we associate preposterously with kings and queens, emperors and empresses, and notabilities of all sorts? Do we not nightly jumble events and personages and times and places, as these do daily? Are we not sometimes troubled by our own sleeping inconsistencies, and do we not vexedly try to account for them or excuse them, just as these do sometimes in respect of their waking delusions? Said an afflicted man to me, when I was last in a hospital like this, "Sir, I can frequently fly." I was half ashamed to reflect that so could

108

BIOGRAPHICAL EXCURSION

I—by night. Said a woman to me on the same occasion, "Queen Victoria frequently comes to dine with me, and her Majesty and I dine off peaches and maccaroni in our night-gowns, and his Royal Highness the Prince Consort does us the honour to make a third on horseback in a Field-Marshal's uniform." Could I refrain from reddening with consciousness when I remembered the amazing royal parties I myself had given (at night), the unaccountable viands I had put on table, and my extraordinary manner of conducting myself on those distinguished occasions? I wonder that the great master who knew everything, when he called Sleep the death of each day's life, did not call Dreams the insanity of each day's sanity.

The "great master who knew everything" is of course Shakespeare, and the allusion is to Macbeth's account of the murder of Duncan:

> Methought I heard a voice cry, "Sleep no more!
> Macbeth does murder sleep,"—the innocent sleep,
> Sleep that knits up the ravell'd sleave of care,
> The death of each day's life, sore labour's bath,
> Balm of hurt minds, great nature's second course,
> Chief nourisher in life's feast.[33]

The interest in this passage for readers of *Bleak House* lies not so much in Dickens's fascinations with dreams and insanity, sleeping and waking in themselves—although of course those interests are fully registered in the novel—as in his fascination with the relations among them. It is *not* that sleep that is the death of each day's life, innocent, able to knit the ravelled sleave of care, and the balm of hurt minds that preoccupies him, but rather the sort of murdered sleep and waking dreaming that are represented in the life by his own Night Walks and in the novel by all those instances of trances and trancelike states that we have enumerated, and indeed also by the novel's allusions to *Macbeth* apropos, especially, of Lady Dedlock. It is, in other words, the sort of double state in which two kinds of consciousness simultaneously operate, and the sort of state, moreover, that I have referred to as an elaboration of "the romantic side of familiar things."

We can see this interest at the center too of an essay which really is a companion piece to "Night Walks," called "Lying Awake" and written in fact when Dickens was writing *Bleak House.* [34] It too probably refers to the two-week-long period of insomnia that accompanied his father's death; but in any case, "Night Walks" takes up where "Lying Awake" leaves off, for the latter essay describes the kind of state that led Dickens to leave his bed in the first place, and that is a state, as we might have guessed, of waking dreaming. Dickens begins by telling us he is "broad awake," but soon his mind begins to wander and the train of "association of ideas," at first willed and self-conscious, becomes fluid and visionary. But as the will relaxes, the visions become terrifying and the train "disagreeable." Dickens keeps falling half-asleep, being frightened by horrible visions, suddenly waking up fully with a start, willing his thoughts to more pleasant things once again, then slipping into a half-sleep again, and so on. Finally his visions are all of death: the Mannings' execution (significant, of course, in connection with Mlle. Hortense), corpses in the Paris Morgue, "a man with his throat cut, dashing towards me as I lie awake!" It is too much to bear:

> I had proceeded thus far, when I found I had been lying
> awake so long that the very dead began to awake too, and to

crowd into my thoughts most sorrowfully. Therefore, I resolved to lie awake no more, but to get up and go out for a night walk—which resolution was an acceptable relief to me, as I dare say it may prove now to a great many more.

But as readers of "Night Walks" will know, if wandering about the streets of London throughout the night provides "acceptable relief," it can hardly be said to solve the problem, for on his nightly tours Dickens is almost as much a prey to his own un- pleasant imaginings as he is when lying awake. In both in- stances he is still a victim of murdered sleep.

Indeed, the same quotation from *Macbeth* he adduces in "Night Walks" occurs to him while lying awake:

> I made up my mind to think a little about Sleep; which I no sooner did than I whirled off in spite of myself to Drury Lane Theatre, and there saw a great actor and dear friend of mine (whom I had been thinking of in the day) playing Macbeth, and heard him apostrophising "the death of each day's life," as I have heard him many a time, in the days that are gone.[35]

Psychoanalytically inclined critics will have little difficulty in coming up with an account of why *Macbeth* should have been so much in Dickens's thoughts at this time: *Macbeth* is, after all about regicide, but the play itself recognizes the close rela- tionship, indeed, the psychological equivalence, between that crime and parricide. Dickens, it can well be argued, reacts to his father's death in very much the way that his own fictional murderers react to their crimes after their doing of the deed, for Dickensian murderers are also among the houseless Night- Walkers in his works. But then any reader of Dickens's life

111

knows about the profundity of his ambivalence about his father, his intense admiration and emulation of his father's imagination and theatricality contrasted with his intense humiliation in and hatred of his father's irresponsibility.[36]

This psychoanalytic interpretation of murderous feelings on Dickens's part against his father, however, is one that we may pass over quickly. It does not greatly advance what we have already discovered in, for example, Tulkinghorn's murder, although it does help perhaps to confirm what our reading has told us—that Dickens has in murdering Tulkinghorn struck a blow against Esther's guilty past, the guilty past of her parents, and the forces that would, by cultivating the power that comes from holding the secret, sustain the guilt, at the same time that he has, as it were, displaced Mlle. Hortense's guilt onto Lady Dedlock and even, to some degree, Esther. More significant for our purposes, I think, is that we have found in "Night Walks" and "Lying Awake" the interest in double states of consciousness that informs the whole ambience of *Bleak House*. And it does seem to me both legitimate and helpful to relate such double states to John Dickens's death in particular, and the deaths of fathers in general, for the dominant gloom of *Bleak House* has much in common with the state of mourning, in which we find ourselves at once grieving for a past we know we cannot recover and unable (and unwilling) to give up that past. The state of mourning, in other words, itself involves a conflict between two competing frames of reference, which is why it is so psychologically dangerous and so paralyzing. It is a state of suspended animation, and a state in which our thoughts helplessly repeat themselves in patterns of frightening circularity. It is very much like the state of being in Chancery or the state of being in *Bleak House*. And it is a state in which we become highly susceptible to feelings of uncanniness.

Being in mourning for one's father of course not only is apt to intensify the usual emotional dilemmas of mourning, but adds to them a unique dimension. The deaths of parents, especially parents who loom so large in their children's lives as John Dickens had, come as positively cosmic events that seem to make the whole universe reel—after all, we create the universe originally in their image.

IV

Viewed in this way, *Bleak House* should look more like a typically Victorian statement about the loss of faith than it has to most critics. In fact there is much that relates *Bleak House* with the greatest Victorian statement of mourning and loss of faith, Tennyson's *In Memoriam*, which was published just the year before Dickens began work on *Bleak House*, and which has provided Dickens, I believe, with yet another source for his novel. But what, among other things, obscures both the influence of the Tennyson poem and the novel's pervasive sense of what we have come to refer to as the death of God is that the feeling of cosmic loss in *Bleak House* is located in a very real social institution, the Court of Chancery, and thus many critics have read the cosmic references simply as Dickens's way of intensifying his point, which is social satire. The social satire is quite real, but the relationship between Chancery and the cosmic imagery that surrounds it should be read as working in two ways. The chaos of the novel's first page of course "stands for" what Chancery does to people in mid-nineteenth-century England. But what Chancery does to people in mid-nineteenth-century England also "stands for" Chaos. We cannot finally distinguish between the symbol and the thing symbolized. It is this double-edgedness of the symbology of *Bleak House* too that figures of course as part of the novel's strategy of dwelling on "the romantic side of familiar things" or maintaining us in a state of continual peripety. As we view Chancery, we can never be sure whether it is the familiar institution or the romantic, symbolic conception of it that we are seeing—because it is always both together.[37]

Several things in the novel in fact are apt to obscure its mourning state from us, and another of them has to do with Esther. In particular, it has to do with the quality in Esther that has irritated so many readers: I mean her busybody cheerfulness, as embodied, say, in her constant jingling and shaking of her little bundle of household keys. Esther's insistent cheerfulness grates on many modern readers, and the reason for this is not, I think, so much that we misunderstand Esther as that we understand her too well. For what I call her busybody cheerfulness can only be understood as a reaction against mourning and grief, and as an intentional effort to overcome them. We in the twentieth century do not like the reaction because we do not like even to admit to ourselves that we mourn or that we grieve. As Philippe Ariès has shown, death has replaced sex as our great taboo, and this is especially true not so much of the uneducated as of the educated class.[38] We love to dwell on the gloomy side of *Bleak House* and of all the later Dickens, but paradoxically we want also to hold the gloom at a safe distance, and then we fall rather into the habits of those who have viewed Chancery at a distance and "have been insensibly tempted into a loose way of letting bad things alone to take their own bad course, and a loose belief that if the world go wrong, it was, in some off-hand manner, never meant to go right" (1). More willing than we are to give way to the intense experience of despair, Dickens felt more urgency about bringing it to an end.

That Esther stands as Dickens's novelistic antidote for morbidity ought to be plain enough from reading *Bleak House*. And that her voice is one of many Dickens himself spoke with in private life is plain from a letter we have of his written in 1850 to a young Danish lady named Emmely Gotschalk, evidently morbidly involved in reading and "sad meditation." "The world is not a dream," Dickens writes her, "but a reality, of which we are the chief part, and in which we must be up and doing something." The letter concludes:

> Be earnest—earnest—in life's reality and do not let your life, which has a purpose in it—every life upon earth has—fly by while you are brooding over mysteries.
>
> The mystery is not here, but far beyond the sky. The preparation for it, is in doing duty. Our Saviour did not sit down in this world and muse, but labored and did good. In your small domestic sphere, you may do as much good as an Emperor can do in his. [39]

Clearly there is a good deal of Esther in Dickens's voice here. But Dickens also could write with quite another voice to John Forster. In the middle of writing *Bleak House*, he speculates to his friend about life that "*this* is all a dream, may be, and death will wake us." [40] *Bleak House*, as we have seen, embraces both positions; but if it is Esther's position that wins out, the position of duty and of that Charity which begins at home, it is not owing to any organically necessary cause. Esther represents faith, to be sure, but not exactly the faith of belief so much as the belief of will. The crisis of faith that occurs with *Bleak House* is resolved, that is to say, not with a religious vision of salvation, but with an essentially secular effort of individual will. *Bleak House,* we could say, is one of the first examples we have of the late Victorian doctrine of the will to believe.

V

The themes of the work are the themes of the life: that is the most general point of this biographical excursion. And it is a point that will, I hope, lead some of my readers to go back and read the life with new interest. In John Forster and Edgar Johnson we have two excellent tellers of the life. We need more critics of it.

I have, I should emphasize, in the space that I have allowed myself here, really only begun to examine the interrelatedness of the life and the work. We have opened Mrs. Jellyby's closet only a little way, and let only a few things come tumbling out. Let me in conclusion suggest a few of the things that remain in the closet.

What remains is very like what we have let out of it—which is why we can afford to leave so much behind. There is first of all another death Dickens had to mourn only two weeks after the death of his father, and that is the death of his infant daughter, Dora Annie, which was very sudden. Her death came naturally as more of a shock to Dickens than even the death of his father and led him into a period of intense, if brief, isolation.[41] The record Dickens has left us in the life of the effects of this double bereavement is very brief. To his old friend Thomas Mitton he writes a week after Dora Annie's death:

> I have been in trouble, or I should have written to you sooner. My wife has been, and is, far from well. My poor father's death caused me much distress. I came to London last Monday to preside at a public dinner—played with little Dora, my youngest child, before I went, and was told when I left the chair that she had died in a moment. I am quite happy again, but I have undergone a good deal.[42]

The note that is sounded here is again very much like the note of grief that is sounded again and again in *Bleak House*. The closing sentence of the letter, in particular, might very well serve as the close of Esther's Narrative.

More germane to "the romantic side of familiar things," perhaps, is Dickens's interest in dreams, mesmerism, and indeed psychology in all its sensational aspects. The history of that interest is far too long and involved to be told here, but what emerges from a study of it is very much like what emerges from a reading of "Night Walks" and "Lying Awake"—or a reading of *Bleak House*: we see there again at the center Dickens's fascination with paradoxical and double states of consciousness—the mesmeric trance is often referred to by him, following the preferred usage of his friend and family physician, John Elliotson, as "sleepwaking"—and transitional states of consciousness.[43] Indeed, taking off from Steven Marcus's discussion of the two scenes in *Oliver Twist* that involve trances, which he connects with a scene in the blacking warehouse from the autobiographical fragment, it is possible for us to construct an intricate and intriguing psychoanalytic account of how Dickens's fascination with these states came about, and that account further connects the fascination with Dickens's feelings about his father. I hope soon to publish that account, too, but again, its conclusions will confirm what we have already learned rather than add anything essential to it—at least for the literary critic if not for the biographer or psychohistorian.

Dickens's fascination with paradoxical states of consciousness is of course as fully recorded in the work as in the life. It is especially pronounced in *Oliver* and in the two novels that appeared in *Master Humphrey's Clock, The Old Curiosity Shop* and *Barnaby Rudge.* It is especially pronounced, that is to say, in the novels in which Dickens's concern with houselessness is especially pronounced. It crops up, however, in some form or other and with more or less intensity in all the novels. My concern with *Bleak House* has been to show that that interest ought to be viewed not so much as a gothic footnote to Dickens's career as centrally connected with the Dickens imagination—as being an essential characteristic of it.

I want to close this biographical excursion with one further example of how Dickens's imagination works and how material from the life and work so insistently and uncannily resonate with one another. My example comes from one of Dickens's overtly autobiographical works—from a work, that is to say, which belongs strictly speaking neither to the work nor to the life, but to both together, *Pictures from Italy.*

Passing on his way to a holiday in Genoa through the Rhone Valley, Dickens stops at Avignon to do some sightseeing:

Hard by the cathedral stands the ancient Palace of the Popes, of which one portion is now a common jail, and another a noisy barrack: while gloomy suites of state apartments, shut up and deserted, mock their own old state and glory, like the embalmed bodies of kings. But we neither went there, to see state rooms, nor soldiers' quarters, nor a common jail, though we dropped some money into a prisoners' box outside, whilst the prisoners, themselves, looked through the iron bars, high up, and watched us eagerly. We went to see the ruins of the dreadful rooms in which the Inquisition used to sit.

A little, old, swarthy woman, with a pair of flashing black eyes,—proof that the world hadn't conjured down the devil within her, though it had had between sixty and seventy years to do it in,—came out of the Barrack Cabaret, of which she was the keeper, with some large keys in her hands, and marshalled us the way that we should go. How she told us, on the way, that she was a Government Officer (*concierge du palais apostolique*), and had been, for I don't know how many years; . . . and how she was the best of dungeon demonstrators; and how she had resided in the palace from an infant,—had been born there, if I recollect right,—I needn't relate. But such a fierce, little, rapid, sparkling, energetic she-devil I never beheld. She was alight and flaming, all the time. Her action was violent in the extreme. She never spoke, without stopping expressly for the purpose. She stamped her feet, clutched us by the arms, flung herself into all attitudes, hammered against walls with her keys, for mere emphasis: now whispered as if the Inquisition were there still: now shrieked as if she were on the rack herself; and had a mysterious, hag-like way with her forefinger, when approaching the remains of some new horror—looking back and walking stealthily, and making horrible grimaces—that might alone have qualified her to walk up and down a sick man's counterpane, to the exclusion of all other figures, through a whole fever.[44]

The tour itself is horrible enough, with the Goblin accompanying her demonstration of "La Salle de la Question" and all its attendant machines of torture with suitable cries and groans, and melodramatically flinging open a trap-door in the floor that reveals an "Infernal Well," the climactic attraction of the tour, the vaults of "les oubliettes de l'Inquisition." It all leaves Dickens positively dazed:

> I walked round the building on the outside, in a sort of dream. . . . The immense thickness and giddy height of the walls, the enormous strength of the massive towers, the great extent of the building, its gigantic proportions, frowning aspect, and barbarous irregularity, awaken awe and wonder. The recollection of its opposite old uses: an impregnable fortress, a luxurious palace, a horrible prison, a place of torture, the court of the Inquisition: at one and the same time, a house of feasting, fighting, religion, and blood: gives to every stone in its huge form a fearful interest, and imparts new meaning to its incongruities. [45]

Several things in these passages ought to strike by now familiar notes, above all, of course, the dreamlike state into which Dickens is thrown not only by the sight of these horrors but also by the profound incongruities of the palace's "opposite old uses," which raises again the whole theme of houses. The very fact that Dickens here is taking a tour might also put us in mind of the theme of houses and, more, the vast number of tours that occur in *Bleak House*—not simply the tours that are given by the third person narrator of Chancery and the fashionable world, but the many tours given by characters in the novel for our and one another's benefit. The second number consists of nothing but tours: Krook's tour of his shop, Miss Flite's of her apartment (5), John Jarndyce's tour of Bleak House (6), and Rosa's and Mrs. Rouncewell's tour of Chesney Wold (7). And there are many more. There is Mrs. Pardiggle's tour of the brickmaker's (8), the tour Jo gives Lady Dedlock of the site of Nemo's lodgings, the inquest, and of his burying-ground (12), and the tour Boythorn gives of the grounds of Chesney Wold (18). There is the tour Krook gives to Tony Jobling of Nemo's room (20), the tour Bucket gives Snagsby of Tom-all-Alone's (22), the tour Mr. Jarndyce and Esther take of the Necketts' lodgings, guided in part by Charley and in part by Mr. Gridley (15), the "grand tour" Sir Leicester gives his cousins of Chesney Wold (28), and so on. The kind of building the Goblin is showing is relevant to *Bleak House* as well, for the Palace of the Popes is rather like a weird conflation of Chancery and Chesney Wold. Chancery is, of course, for Dickens very much the modern counterpart of the Inquisition—which was, after all, a court. Smaller details reverberate as well. The "Infernal Well" in the Palace echoes the "kind of well in the floor" of Krook's shop (5) which, of course, also is an image that is repeated in the window-seat in Ada's room at Bleak House; and Chancery has its "well" of solicitors (1). Furthermore, a number of details about the Goblin of Avignon recall details of characters (some of whom are tour-givers) in *Bleak House*. The Goblin is rather like a demonic version of Mrs. Rouncewell, whom she resembles in age. Her "mysterious way with her forefinger," however, points rather to Mr. Bucket and his famous forefinger, while it is a nightmarishly inverted image of Esther that is suggested by the bundle of keys she jangles for emphasis.

Only one detail, however, clinches for me as positive the connection between these passages and *Bleak House*. With her "flashing black eyes," her stamping feet, and her being in general "such a fierce, little, rapid, sparkling, energetic she-devil" as Dickens had never beheld, the character in *Bleak House* she

121

most resembles—excepting only her age—is Mlle. Hortense, whose "black eyes [dart] fire," who stamps her feet menacingly (54) and who is like a "She-Wolf imperfectly trained" (12). Mlle. Hortense, moreover, is not only a fellow countrywoman of the Goblin's: like her, she is a native specifically of Avignon (12).

It is not remarkable that Mlle. Hortense should have an original in the crazy little old woman who had guided Dickens through the Palace of the Popes at Avignon seven years before. (It may be coincidence—and then again it may not—that Dickens places the events of the novel as occurring seven years before Esther sets them down in her narrative [67].) What *is* remarkable, however, is that the Goblin carries with her so much of the rest of the novel as well. Tracing sources often leads to dead ends: we locate an original and then are left with the question, So what? Tracing sources so often proves fruitless because, we assume, it is only in the creative, synthesizing imagination that they are given meaning and significance. In the case of the Goblin, however, the situation is in some ways reversed: the Goblin has a more obvious connection with Chancery in its Inquisitorial capacities than does Mlle. Hortense—though we have found other strands in the novel that do indeed connect her with it. To put it another way, we can say that rather than synthesizing its sources, *Bleak House* in some way decomposes them. Thus it is that Mrs. Rouncewell, Bucket, Esther, and so on can be read as characters who all have been transfigured out of the figure of the Goblin.

I have already spoken of *Bleak House* as a kind of extended gloss on the idea of causal relations—as though Dickens had that phrase in mind throughout the writing of the novel and was

122

continuously spinning out all its permutations and implications. Here with the Goblin we have found another nexus of ideas that seems similarly to preoccupy him and to serve as a continual source of inspiration. If we were to follow the Goblin's trail further we would discover a good many more such constellations of apparently seminal ideas and images. Specifically, the Goblin's trail leads to Genoa, where Dickens has a dream about Mary Hogarth, his beloved sister-in-law who had died in his arms seven (that number will keep coming up) years before. In that dream there figure prominently Dickens's horror and hatred of Catholicism—thus another connection with the Goblin—and the image of Mary, who comes to him as a mysteriously veiled and hooded figure: a figure like Lady Dedlock, in short, or Mlle. Hortense, or Esther. But here we shall let Dickens continue on his holiday, while we bring our own excursion to a close.

CHAPTER FIVE

THE NOVEL AND THE NOVEL: REALISM AND THE ROMANCE OF THE FAMILIAR

Fog everywhere.
—*Bleak House*, chapter 1

I

I HOPE that the extended gloss I have offered on the phrase "the romantic side of familiar things" has by now been justified by my demonstration that *Bleak House* itself can be seen as an extended gloss on Dickens's remark. It remains for us to discover what our reading of that novel has to tell us about the rest of Dickens's work and, further, what it has to tell us about the general history of the English novel.

The "romantic side" of things in *Bleak House* reflects, as we have seen, an interest of Dickens's in things bizarre that runs throughout his life and that has, under other names, long been recognized as an important component of his character, and, indeed, of the age of his childhood and youth. To the literary historian, "the romantic side" of Dickens might more properly be known as the Gothic side, for the influence of the Gothic novelists—most importantly, I think, Lewis and Hogg—is an obvious strain that can be traced through all the works.[1] More important for this study, however, is that the *tension* between the "romantic" and the "familiar" that Dickens sets up in *Bleak House* is also a lifelong interest. Hillis Miller's essay on *Sketches by Boz* and *Oliver Twist*, cited above, shows how this is true at the very beginning of Dickens's career,[2] and of course it is much more obviously the case at the very end of the career with *Edwin Drood* and Jasper's opium trances and presumed double states of consciousness.

Most commonly, that tension is explicitly presented by Dickens in the works before and after *Bleak House* in various states of confusion experienced by many characters. Here are two early and typical passages, from *The Old Curiosity Shop* and *Barnaby Rudge*.

> How every circumstance of her short, eventful life, came thronging into her mind, as they travelled on! Slight incidents, never thought of or remembered until now; faces, seen once and ever since forgotten; words, scarcely heeded at the time; scenes, of a year ago and those of yesterday, mixing up and linking themselves together; familiar places shaping themselves out in the darkness from things which, when approached, were, of all others, the most remote and most unlike them; sometimes, a strange confusion in her mind relative to the occasion of her being there, and the place to which she was going, and the people she was with; and imagination suggesting remarks and questions which sounded so plainly in her ears, that she would start, and turn, and be almost tempted to reply;—all the fancies and

contradictions common in watching and excitement and restless change of place, beset the child. (*The Old Curiosity Shop*, 43)

The locksmith, however, . . . still jogged on, half sleeping and half waking, when a loud cry at no great distance ahead, roused him with a start.

For a moment or two he looked about him like a man who had been transported to some strange country in his sleep, but soon recognizing familiar objects, rubbed his eyes lazily and might have relapsed again, but that the cry was repeated. . . . (*Barnaby Rudge*, 3)

We have already met many instances of this kind of trancelike confusion in *Bleak House*, of course—in Snagsby's desperate confusion about Bucket and Jo, for example, and most centrally in Esther's smallpox delirium. But it is interesting to see that even in these very early passages the confusion explicitly takes the form of a tension between the "familiar" and the "strange." In *Bleak House* that tension belongs not just to its characters but to the reader and to the very novel itself; and this is true to an extraordinary degree. No other book of Dickens's maintains that tension so insistently and continuously. If we are interested in saying what distinguishes *Bleak House* from the rest of Dickens's work, what belongs to it peculiarly and centrally, then we can point to that tension, which is there as the central organizing (or perhaps disorganizing) principle from beginning to end, the principle that gives the novel its distinct feeling and personality. But in a larger sense, it is also the tension that informs all of Dickens's prose. *Bleak House* is different because it embodies more completely than any other of Dickens's works a characteristically Dickensian conflict. All of Dickens's *prose* dwells on "the romantic side of familiar things," but only in *Bleak House* does the entire *narrative* dwell there as well, and only in *Bleak House* has Dickens pushed the tension to its greatest limits; so that we can say that in *Bleak House* the tension leaves us hovering on the edge of horror and nightmare. In *Bleak House*, the tension is so insistent that it threatens to get out of control and to fling us into what William James (speaking of his own religious crisis) calls "that pit of insecurity beneath the surface of life." [3]

This is not necessarily to argue that *Bleak House* is Dickens's greatest novel, though it is to argue that it is in this one way his most completely Dickensian. Other novels, certainly, are most completely Dickensian in other ways. Obviously the extremist who finds none of the books after *Pickwick* entirely satisfactory has his point, although obviously, too, he is missing a great deal.

Critics nowadays are fond of speaking of Dickens's development. The development is very real, but does not entail a growth from the lesser to the greater so much as a growth from one kind of greatness to another. In its own way, *Pickwick* is not only fully achieved, but achieves something very great, and if we tend today to believe that *Our Mutual Friend* is a greater novel, it is not, I hope, in the way that we believe *The Tempest* is greater than *The Two Gentlemen of Verona*. Dickens wrote very few books that are not fully achieved and that are not great achievements, and he left us no clear masterpiece. That is why I do not want to speak of the greatness or the purity of Dickensianness of *Bleak House* at the expense of the other novels. But I do mean to speak of that organized and organizing tension we have been examining in such detail in *Bleak House* as exem-

128

plary because it is I believe central to the tradition of the novel, and I do mean to argue, therefore, that *Bleak House* is in this way Dickens's most novelistic novel. To see how this is so, we shall have to venture out of the fog of *Bleak House* and into a fog of another kind.

II

The whole question of what is novelistic is of course extraordinarily vexed. I suppose that the Dickens novel most often cited, explicitly or implicitly, as his most novelistic in the sense of fitting most comfortably into the tradition of the novel, is *Great Expectations.* Such a judgment already, of course, implies a fairly specific notion of that tradition—and one I shall argue against accepting; it is a notion founded chiefly upon criteria of plausibility and complexity of character and, above all, of "realism," a notion that tends to select as among the great novelists Richardson, Jane Austen, Thackeray, George Eliot, say, over Defoe, Fielding, Smollett, Emily Brontë, and Dickens. I say "tends" because inevitably such critics, working with quite similar explicit criteria, and quite different implicit ones, select different novelists for their lists of the greats. Virginia Woolf brings Defoe in, for example, and F. R. Leavis throws him out, only to have Ian Watt march him back in again. And yet all these critics share notions of the novel that have to do with "realism." The problem, of course, is that none of them quite agree upon what constitutes reality.

Ian Watt's definition of "formal realism," the novel's distinguishing "narrative method," is perhaps the most concise definition of what is characteristic of the novel that we have had from any of these critics I have broadly classed together as proponents of "realism." Watt writes:

> The narrative method whereby the novel embodies this circumstantial view of life may be called its formal realism; formal, because the term realism does not here refer to any special literary doctrine or purpose, but only to a set of narrative procedures which are so commonly found together in the novel, and so rarely in other literary genres, that they may be regarded as typical of the form itself. Formal realism, in fact, is the narrative embodiment of a premise that Defoe and Richardson accepted very literally, but which is implicit in the novel form in general: the premise, or primary convention, that the novel is a full and authentic report of human experience, and is therefore under an obligation to satisfy its reader with such details of the story as the individuality of the actors concerned, the particulars of the times and places of their actions, details which are presented through a more largely referential use of language than is common in other literary forms.[4]

Watt's definition has justly come to be a classic for the proponents of realism not only because it appears in one of the most intelligent and informative books ever written about the early novel, but also because it is at once wonderfully concise and takes in a great deal of territory. F. R. Leavis's ideas about what constitutes a good or great novel are a good deal more complicated and narrow, but obviously fit within Watt's definition. Nevertheless, as broad as it is, Watt's definition already contains in that phrase "a full and authentic account of human experience" a bias for the sort of novel George Eliot writes, say, and a bias against the sort of novel Dickens writes. Watt's definition, to be sure, is highly sophisticated in that it takes into account the fact that *no* "realism" finally is *real* "realism." "Formal realism" is, he tells us, "of course, like the rules of evidence, only a convention; and there is no reason why the report on human life which is presented by it should be in fact any truer than those presented through the very different conventions of other literary genres." [5] Yet the bias in favor of this particular convention remains essential to Watt's definition, as it does to many writers on the novel.

Realism is today under heavy attack, of course. What is for Watt merely a qualification of his definition can be taken instead as the first axiom of a quite different and anti-realistic view of the novel. If no realism is a real realism, then, it is argued, there is no point in talking about realism at all. Fictional worlds, no matter how congruent with the conventional view of reality, remain as much fictional worlds as the most far-flung fantasies of disordered imagination. Kafka tells the truth as fully as Flaubert. Such a view deflates not only realism, indeed, but any number of distinctions we may draw among all kinds of narrative writing in prose. It erases, that is to say, the line between fiction on the one hand, and biography and history on the other. Everything ultimately becomes fiction, including, I suppose, criticism itself. Works of art are to be studied not in relation to the worlds they purport to portray, but in relation to themselves. Judgments about value, finally, have to do with a work's truthfulness to itself and to the rules and conventions it establishes and accepts for itself.

The debate between the realists and anti-realists has left what we like to call *the* theory of the novel in a shambles. There is today no theory of the novel, but there are many theories of the novel. Indeed, the situation now seems in many ways but a repetition of the inconclusiveness of debates that have been going on since the very beginnings of the novel; and perhaps it would be more accurate to say that today's debate has simply failed to clean up the shambles rather than that it has created a new one. It will be worth our while to look briefly at the shambles' origins.

III

The Preface to Defoe's *Moll Flanders*, reckoned by many to be the first English novel, takes us at once into the problem. The Preface begins:

> The world is so taken up of late with novels and romances, that it will be hard for a private history to be taken for genuine, where the names and other circumstances of the persons are concealed; and on that account we must be content to leave the reader to pass his own opinion upon the ensuing sheets, and take it just as he pleases.

It is nicely ambiguous, and might seem not to have anything to tell us about the kind of work he is writing—except perhaps indirectly that we shouldn't believe what novelists have to say about themselves. What is often taken to be the first English novel begins with a disclaimer that it is a novel at all, and presents itself instead as a true "history." Defoe, of course, was lying on both points, but the lie is a significant—that is to say, meaningful—one.

We can immediately see how the novel's claim to be a genuine account of real experiences fits neatly into Watt's definition of formal realism. Clearly, if Defoe is going to make good his claim he is going to have to play out Watt's premise skilfully and to the letter. But in indicating the great obstacle to his book's being taken as a genuine account of real experiences, Defoe also points to quite another premise about realistic fiction. Even true accounts, Defoe tells us, *look like* "novels and romances," excepting that names "and other circumstances" have been changed. It is but a very short step indeed from this perception to the modern notion that historians and other chroniclers of real events need to be regarded as novelists. The point that to my mind needs making about this first sentence of *Moll Flanders* is that it contains *both* views of fiction: on the one hand, Defoe keeps strictly within the bounds of formal realism as later defined by Watt, and, on the other, he takes as given the identity of narrative methods between his supposedly true account and those of patently untrue and fantastic "novels and romances." It is not in its formal realism that fiction can be distinguished from nonfiction, Defoe is saying, but solely on the basis of empirically verifiable facts, which necessarily lie wholly outside the text. And if we go along with Defoe on this, then we have to say that for the literary critic who is not willing also to assume the role of the historian, there can be no way of distinguishing between a novel and an "authentic report of human experience." From a strictly literary point of view, the novel therefore does not exist.

Of course, we are all historians in practice, and are all willing to accept the judgment of other historians; thus we judge what is fiction and what is not. Nevertheless, the fact that we cannot distinguish novels except by reference to their specific (as opposed to general) truthfulness, to their property of fictionality, gives them a special place in the list of genres. And it is a troubling place. Watt himself seems to be troubled when trying to pin down the distinction between the novel and earlier forms of narrative, for he recognizes—as does Defoe in our quotation from *Moll Flanders*—that "formal realism" was not entirely the invention of the early novelists. He writes:

> In the strictest sense, of course, formal realism was not discovered by Defoe and Richardson; they only applied it much more completely than had been done before. Homer, for example, as Carlyle pointed out, shared with them that outstanding 'clearness of sight' which is manifested in the 'detailed, ample and lovingly exact' descriptions that abound in their works; and there are many passages in later fiction, from *The Golden Ass* to *Aucassin and Nicolette*, from Chaucer to Bunyan, where the characters, their actions and their environment are presented with a particularity as authentic as that in any eighteenth-century novel. But there is an important difference: in Homer and in earlier prose fiction these passages are relatively rare, and tend to stand out from the surrounding narrative; the total literary structure was not consistently oriented in the direction of formal realism, and the plot especially, which was usually traditional and often highly improbable, was in direct conflict with its premises. Even when previous writers had overtly professed a wholly realistic aim, as did many seventeenth-century writers, they did not pursue it wholeheartedly. La Calprenède, Richard Head, Grimmelshausen, Bunyan, Aphra Ben, Furetière, to mention only a few, had all asserted that their fictions were literally true; but their preparatory asseverations are no more convincing than the very similar ones to be found in most works of medieval hagiography. The aim of verisimilitude had not been deeply enough assimilated in either case to bring about the full rejection of all the non-realistic conventions that governed the genre.[6]

THE NOVEL AND THE NOVEL

Watt's paragraph is worth quoting in full because it is here I think that we can see the theory of formal realism at its weakest. What distinguishes the novel from earlier forms of narrative, Watt says, is that novels are "consistently oriented in the direction of formal realism," instead of being only sporadically oriented toward formal realism. This would make for a weak definition of the novel at the very outset, even if it were true that novelists follow up the premises of formal realism more consistently than their predecessors. Watt overlooks first of all the point he has just made: that formal realism is a convention that depends upon a particular age's criteria for the credibility of evidence. Of course, by eighteenth-century standards, the evidence that Homer or the authors of the saints' lives presents is scarcely credible. But if we accept that the premises of formal realism are subject to historical change, then we have to say that Homer and the authors of saints' lives are all consistently oriented toward what in their times would be accepted as formally realistic. In fact, we have not one bit of evidence that Homer or the authors of saints' lives did not themselves believe in the literal truth of what they were recording—which is more certainly than can be said of Defoe or Richardson.

The theory of formal realism, indeed, simply does not work by the time we come to Fielding, who offers us no serious pretense at all about the factuality of his books. He not only is making stories up, but also admits it to the reader. In fact, Fielding flaunts it before the reader. The famous introductory chapters to the book divisions of *Joseph Andrews* and *Tom Jones* are essays in how to make up good stories, and surely there is a large irony in the great emphasis Fielding lays in these chapters on plausibility and verisimilitude. He believes, to be sure, in these qualities as real virtues; but he believes in them and is interested in them as real virtues in clearly imaginary books—which again is something quite different from what we find in the Homeric epics or in saints' lives. What delights Fielding is not verisimilitude plain and simple, but the play between the plainly "real" and the plainly "fictional." And on this he quotes (in the first chapter of the eighth book of *Tom Jones*) no less an authority than Pope: "As a genius of the highest rank observes in his 5th chapter of the *Bathos*, 'The great art of all poetry is to mix truth with fiction; in order to join the credible with the surprizing.' " This principle Fielding self-consciously extends to the "new province of writing" of which he regards himself as the "founder." [7]

In his own way, Fielding poses as much of a problem as Defoe. Defoe asserts that his history is true, but asserts too that it looks like nothing so much as "novels and romances." Fielding asserts his continuity with past literary traditions, but asserts too that he is founding "a new province of writing." The problem for the literary critic in each case remains the same: what then *is* novel about the novel?

IV

By making explicit what is hidden in Defoe's remarks—the fact that what is presented really is fictional—Fielding points the way to an answer. Novels consist of made up stories—stories, moreover, newly made up for the occasion. In that sense they are literally "novel." But the word "novel" in the eighteenth century also denotes two other and quite opposite things we

136

have already seen are relevant to the novel as genre. "Novel" can mean a bit of news (as does its French cognate, *nouvelles*); it can also mean a lie. In its application to the novel as genre, it means, I think, all three things: novels are newly made up stories (i.e., lies) presented as if they were the news. Indeed, both as lies and as pretended news they generally go beyond previous narratives, which for the most part retell or elaborate upon traditional stories, and for the most part too do not present those stories with the kind of detailed documentation we find even in the newspapers. However, it seems to me that what is most important is that novels always make great and sustained play out of the tension between their manifest fictionality and their pretense at telling the news. Thus Watt's notion of "formal realism" really is essential to the form—except that it always must be put alongside its counterpart, the novel's obvious fictionality.

Clearly the definition I am working toward here differs considerably from the traditional definitions of the form that always keep in mind a distinction between novel and romance. Defoe obviously lumps "novels and romances" together—as does Richardson—and in fact throughout much of the eighteenth century there is an enormous confusion of terminology surrounding the novel. It is not until late in the century, in 1785, that we get a definition of the novel, as distinct from romance, that has now become a classic starting point for theoretical discussions about the novel. The definition is by Clara Reeve:

Euphrasia. . . . The word *Novel* in all languages signifies something new. It was first used to distinguish these works from

137

Romance, though they have lately been confounded together and are frequently mistaken for each other.

Sohpronia. But how will you draw the line of distinction, so as to separate them effectually, and prevent further mistakes?

Euphrasia. I will attempt this distinction, and I presume if it is properly done it will be followed,—If not, you are but where you were before. The Romance is an heroic fable, which treats of fabulous persons and things.—The Novel is a picture of real life and manners, and of the times in which it was written. The Romance in lofty and elevated language, describes what never happened nor is likely to happen.—The Novel gives a familiar relation of such things, as pass every day before our eyes, such as may happen to our friend, or to ourselves; and the perfection of it, is to represent every scene, in so easy and natural a manner, and to make them appear so probable, as to deceive us into a persuasion (at least while we are reading) that all is real, until we are affected by the joys or distresses, of the persons in the story, as if they were our own.[8]

It is a definition, like Watt's (which plainly owes much to it), wonderful for its clarity, but it is a definition, too, that makes I believe an ultimately unhelpful distinction. Everyone will assent, I think, to the proposition that interests in the marvellous on the one hand and the commonplace on the other represent polar tendencies. The question is, can these polar tendencies be so neatly resolved into or equated with two opposite genres? Most critics have in theory said yes, for the distinction between novel and romance remains a live one in much writing about the novel. In practice, however, the distinction breaks down. Scott and Hawthorne, for example, both of whom are self-professed writers of romance, are commonly taught in courses on the novel—and this not only without protest, but necessarily so, for we all recognize that to teach the novel without teaching

Scott, say, would do violence to the history of the genre. In practice, that is to say, the forms continue to be "confounded together," because the theoretical distinction between them is belied by the fact that the tradition of the novel contains within it as an essential part an active tradition of romance. If we stick closely to Watt's or to Clara Reeve's definitions, then we could easily enough teach Defoe and Richardson in courses on the novel, but thereafter we begin to have serious problems—as we have already seen in the case of Fielding—unless we loosen up those criteria considerably. But loosening up the criteria does away with the distinction.

A few writers on the novel have, indeed, done away with the distinction, notably Robert Scholes and Robert Kellogg in *The Nature of Narrative.* After discussing the two opposing tendencies of narrative, what they call the empirical and the fictional, Scholes and Kellogg go on to write:

We have been considering the breakdown of the epic synthesis into two antithetical components. We must now consider briefly the new synthesis in narrative which has been the main development in post-Renaissance narrative literatures. This was a gradual process, beginning at least as early as Boccaccio, but it is most obviously discernible in Europe during the seventeenth and eighteenth centuries. The new synthesis can be seen clearly in a writer like Cervantes, whose great work is an attempt to reconcile powerful empirical and fictional impulses. From the synthesis he effected, the novel emerges as a literary form. The novel is not the opposite of romance, as is usually maintained, but a product of the reunion of the empirical and fictional elements in narrative literature. Mimesis (which tends to short forms like the Character and "slice of life") and history (which can become too scientific and cease to be literature) combine in the novel with romance and fable, even as primitive legend, folktale and sacred myth originally combined in the epic, to produce a great and synthetic literary form. There are signs that in the twentieth century the grand dialectic is about to begin again, and that the novel must yield its place to new forms just as the epic did in ancient times, for it is an unstable compound, inclining always to break down into its constituent elements.[9]

This is an extraordinary passage in the history of writing on the novel, extraordinary for its insight and for the apparent ease with which that insight has been achieved. Unhappily the importance of what is said here does not seem to have registered fully with other writers on the novel—for one thing, perhaps, because it is not even fully registered in the later chapters of *The Nature of Narrative* itself, for another, because it threatens to alter our map of the novel fairly drastically.

On the face of it, the "synthetic" quality of the novel ought to be immediately apparent. Obviously one of the great difficulties we have in defining the novel as a genre is that it is the genre that more than any other absorbs other genres. It absorbs history, drama, journalism, philosophy, the essay, biography and autobiography, letter-writing, and books of travel, as well as the older traditions of epic and romance. And this is perfectly consonant with what we know of the history of the period in which the novel emerges, for it is a period in which the very notion of genre is at once discovered and exploded. I mean by this that it is generally in the seventeenth and eighteenth centuries that genres come to be discovered by writers as forms available for conscious use and change rather than simply as pre-existing forms that must be followed. Genre ceases to mean the way we *must* do things and becomes instead the way things *have been* done and, most importantly, *need not be* done. The genres that are handed down to us can be used, modified, or put aside, for new genres can be invented. This simultaneous discovery and explosion of genre is not, of course, confined to the literary developments that give rise to the novel. It is a process that characterizes much of the literature of the late eighteenth and early nineteenth centuries. In poetry, the *Lyrical Ballads* are a self-conscious expression of that process, as their title itself makes clear. The modern discovery and explosion of genre indeed also forms part of the great modern movement that culminates in political life with the French Revolution: it too is a discovery that has fundamentally to do with the discovery (or invention) of the concept of liberty.

V

To characterize the novel as an unstable, synthesizing genre, always threatening to break down into its component genres, is necessarily to make its own instability a primary characteristic. That is one reason why I think we must add to Scholes and Kellogg's definition a proposition that I have already made: that novels always make great and sustained play out of the tension between their manifest fictionality and their pretense at telling the news—they make play, that is to say, out of the tensions between their component genres. This is not necessarily the case with the other great unstable genre, the epic. For the epic cannot be said to be a synthesizing genre in quite the way that the novel is. The epic is in effect the original genre that gives birth to all other genres, and the tension between those nascent genres—its instability, that is to say—is merely potential. This radical difference between epic and novel is the starting point, in fact, of Georg Lukács' great essay, *The Theory of the Novel.*

Now to make this instability a primary characteristic of the novel very much changes the traditional shape of the history of the novel. In particular, it makes the empirical or realistic tendencies of the novel secondary—or it makes them secondary the more pronounced they become at the expense of the novel's romantic or fictional tendencies; for in our definition the novel is characterized by a sustained tension and play between its empirical and fictional impulses. Among other things that have obscured this for so long is that one of the great myths of the nineteenth century was that "realistic" fiction transcended the demystified category of genre: realism in the minds of its proponents represented not simply another way of writing, but rather the only proper way to write—at least to write novels. Realism became, in other words, paradoxically a genre in the old sense: not a form to be played with, but a form so compelling that it couldn't even be seen as a form, and could be seen only as a necessity and, indeed, as truth. That, after all, is what realism is supposed to mean. It was a myth, moreover, subscribed to in part even by those writers who did not consider themselves realists in the usual sense—like Dickens, for example, whose claim about his narrative in preface after preface is, as he says of Nancy's character (in the preface to the third edition of *Oliver Twist*), that "IT IS TRUE."

But the new shape this definition gives to the novel is not intended to deform the novel out of all recognition, nor to decanonize the realists. If it did, it wouldn't be much of a definition. In spite of the myth of realism, those writers we usually consider novelists remain so, for we can discern in the work even of the most realistic of them precisely that sustained tension and play I have argued is essential to the form. Consider, for a moment, Thackeray, the first novelist to appear during Dickens's career who seriously threatened his supremacy with the critics and with the novelists themselves. In a famous letter he maintains that "the Art of Novels is . . . to convey as strongly as possible the sentiment of reality as opposed to a tragedy or poem, which may be heroical." [10] That wonderful phrase "the sentiment of reality" seems at first glance to convey something very similar to the aim of formal realism—how, indeed, can one convey "the sentiment of reality" without attempting to convince the reader that the book before him is a full and authentic account of human experience? The answer lies in the fact that Thackeray draws his opposition between not the real and the imaginary, but, what is not exactly the same thing, the real and the ideal. Novels, he is saying, must *feel* like real life, and they can achieve this not so much by attention to documentary detail as by remaining true to the way we feel about our lives. No particular pretense about the literal, factual realism of the people portrayed need be made. And in a novel like *Vanity Fair*, no such pretense is in fact made. On the contrary, Thackeray is the nineteenth century's great admirer and imitator of Fielding, and he rubs our noses in the fictionality of his inventions even more insistently than his teacher had done. Consider, for example, his wonderful digression in chapter 6 on the ways in which he might have written about Jos Sedley's love for Becky, or the famous close of the novel, "—Come children, let us shut up the box and the puppets, for the play is played out." Here Thackeray goes a good deal beyond the bounds of formal realism, and further than would a supposed anti-realist like

Dickens, who never betrays the merely imaginary reality of his characters in this ironic way—or in any other. Oddly, Dickens is in fact on the surface of his narrative as true as any of the Victorian novelists to the premises of formal realism. Realists quarrel with Dickens not over his failure to portray his characters as if they were real, but over the fact that such people could never have existed. Indeed, we may be quite sure that had Dickens's narratives been less formally realistic, the quarrel with the realists would have been proportionately less intense.

If the definition of the novel I have been working with is not intended to exclude the realists, clearly it is intended to oust them from the reigning position they have traditionally occupied as the only highly serious practitioners of the genre; and it is intended also to bring back into the fold writers whose works have usually been regarded as peripheral. There is today a good deal of interest in the subgenres that are usually regarded as spinoffs from the central tradition of the novel—in, for example, the Gothic novel in the late eighteenth and early nineteenth centuries, and the mystery novel in the late nineteenth century. My argument is that these forms are not necessarily subgenres at all, but that their interests are centrally novelistic; indeed, we could argue that in both forms there is an attempted return (it need not be a conscious one) and renewal of the novel's crucial instability. This is not to argue, of course, that *The Castle of Otranto* or *The Moonstone* are great novels, but it is to argue not only that they are respectably, but also centrally novelistic; and that may account in part for why critical attention to them has been gradually increasing.

In fact, some of the best early definitions we have of the novel are to be found in writers of Gothic novels and romances.

THE NOVEL AND THE NOVEL

Consider, for example, Horace Walpole's Preface to the second edition of *The Castle of Otranto*. He tells us that the book

> was an attempt to blend the two kinds of romance: the ancient and the modern. In the former, all was imagination and improbability; in the latter, nature is always intended to be, and sometimes has been, copied with success. Invention has not been wanting; but the great resources of fancy have been dammed up, by a strict adherence to common life. But if in the latter species nature has cramped imagination, she did but take her revenge, having been totally excluded from old romances. The actions, sentiments, conversations, of the heroes and heroines of ancient days, were as unnatural as the machines employed to put them in motion.
>
> The author of the following pages thought it possible to reconcile the two kinds. Desirous of leaving the powers of fancy at liberty to expatiate through the realms of invention, and thence of creating more interesting situations, he wished to conduct the mortal agents in his drama according to the rules of probability; in short, to make them think, speak, and act, as it might be supposed mere men and women would do in extraordinary positions.

The "modern" romance is of course the novel, and Walpole here is self-consciously setting out to reform it by fusing its empirical interest with the fictional interest of the ancient romance. It is precisely the project that the definition of the novel we have arrived at assumes, and precisely the project that, we have seen, Fielding sets out for himself. Significantly enough, Walpole understands that the purely empirical interest of the novel is itself largely a fiction, for in the novel, as he drily remarks, "nature is always intended to be, and sometimes has been, copied with success." That perception itself implies an

145

understanding that this new version of the novel that Walpole is inventing in fact derives from the old; it merely recognizes and accepts a truth about the novel that is denied in such usual definitions as Clara Reeve's—a truth that has to do with the *tension* between the real and the imaginary, or the empirical and the fictional, or the commonplace and the marvellous.

Or consider also Sir Walter Scott's thoughts about what constitutes the romantic in historical romance. In the Introduction to *The Fortunes of Nigel,* he writes:

> Lady Mary Wortley Montague has said, with equal truth and taste, that the most romantic region of every country is that where the mountains unite themselves with the plains or lowlands. For similar reasons, it may be in like manner said, that the most picturesque period of history is that when the ancient rough and wild manners of a barbarous age are just becoming innovated upon, and contrasted, by the illumination of increased or revived learning, and the instructions of renewed or reformed religion. The strong contrast produced by the opposition of ancient manners to those which are gradually subduing them, affords the lights and shadows necessary to give effect to a fictitious narrative; and while such a period entitles the author to introduce incidents of a marvellous and improbable character, as arriving out of the turbulence, independence and ferocity, belonging to old habits of violence, still influencing the manners of a people who had yet been lately in a barbarous state; yet, on the other hand, the characters and sentiments of many of the actors may, with the utmost probability, be described with great variety of shading and delineation, which belongs to the newer and more improved period, of which the world has but lately received the light.

Scott, as his famous essay on "Romance" makes plain, accepts the traditional opposition between novel and romance.[11] But here that opposition begins to break down, for what Scott hits upon as the essence of romance is not a simple quality in opposition to the novel's interest in the commonplace and, what he interestingly equates with it, the modern, but rather the fact that romance contains within itself both poles of that opposition. The romantic element in the historical romance is itself therefore characterized by "contrast" and "opposition," and contains within it the traditionally novelistic impulses. And rather than seeking to "reconcile" the opposing poles, as had been Walpole's design, Scott's avowed purpose is to let the imaginative life of the historical romance grow out of the tension between them, so to speak. Scott's definition, in fact, of all the early novelists' (with its emphasis upon contrasting genres and its implicit emphasis, indeed, upon periods of historical instability), comes closest to the definition we have been working with. The only qualification we have to add is that it is a definition that works equally well for historical romance and the novel in general if we only substitute for Scott's specific interest in "the ancient rough and wild manners of a barbarous age" any number of more general interests in "incidents of a marvellous and improbable character." [12]

We could look for novels in which there is no tension between the various polar opposites we have been discussing, all of which resolve themselves into essentially the same tension; or at least we could look for novels in which such tensions generate no significant imaginative life. I think that would be a difficult and unrewarding project. The most obvious place to look would be among the late nineteenth-century heirs to naturalism in England, but even a quick search there shows that we are still on familiar ground. *New Grub Street*, for example, is a fiercely realistic novel, and nothing in it certainly could be said to exceed the most stringent criteria of plausibility or even probability. There is of course the perennial problem of the semi-omniscient third person narrator—a device, it can be argued easily, that implicitly always calls attention to a work's fictionality and that, in so doing, implicitly takes us always beyond the premises of pure formal realism. But we may, for the sake of argument, put that problem aside as a convention so pervasively in use that it has ceased to trouble the most ardent realists. Nevertheless, the tension remains, and glaringly: not formally, to be sure, but thematically. For naturalism is not simply a formal doctrine, but an ideology, and that ideology has to do with the shattering of romantic illusions in the face of reality. *New Grub Street* is of course about the fall of a romantic and the rise of a realist, and because that contrast is made depressing for us, we have to say that the novel, even if only in order to smash romantic illusions, has initially to sustain them as well. Every proponent of naturalism is a romantic at heart, and his ideology depends for its survival on the irrepressibility of romantic illusion, on the irrepressibility, that is to say, of a hope that "incidents of a marvellous and improbable character" may yet be possible. The naturalistic novel, far from being an exception that proves the rule, is no exception at all, and is as much about the clash between ancient romantic and modern realistic beliefs and manners as Scott's historical romances. Of course, various experiments by twentieth-century novelists have pushed the novel further into the realm of realism—as well as further into the realm of fantasy. It may indeed be true, as Scholes and Kellogg suggest, that the novel has by now been decomposed into its component forms. If that is the case, then the novel has lost its central synthesizing tension, and the great age of the novel is now over.

VI

But what, finally, has all this to do with *Bleak House?* Or what has *Bleak House* to do with all this? It should by now be clear that the reading of *Bleak House* I have offered in the earlier chapters of this book has been an extended attempt at reading one novel precisely according to the definition of the novel I have proposed in this last chapter. And while that definition is not wholly new, having been suggested in part by other writers, the attempt to make it the basis of a sustained analysis, to the best of my knowledge, is. The tension that is suggested by Dickens's phrase, "the romantic side of familiar things," and that, we have seen, is embodied in a host of ways by his novel, is I believe the same tension—or family of tensions, perhaps—that is centrally organizing generally in the novel as a form: a family of tensions that is typically expressed in such oppositions as that between the familiar and the strange, the real and the imaginary, the topical and the mythical, the empirical and the fictional, the modern and the ancient, and so on. In my reading of *Bleak House*, I have tried to suggest at once the multiplicity of ways in which we can interpret Dickens's remark, and to show that that multiplicity is at the same time genuinely and successfully encompassed and unified by the phrase and by the book. The point of this last chapter has been to begin to explore the hypothesis that to dwell upon "the romantic side of familiar things" is a formulation that successfully articulates an imaginative project central in all novels.

Even if, in the extreme insistence of its dwelling upon "the romantic side of familiar things," *Bleak House* is a quintessentially novelistic novel, it paradoxically remains, by any standards, an exceptional one. The sustained play that all novels

149

make between the empirical and the fictional or between the real and the ideal is perhaps the chief source of what used to be called the novel's power to amuse its readers. In *Bleak House*, however, the tension is discovered to be deeply problematic. It is as though the novel as a form had gone on from portraying the conflicts of the unstable society that had given it birth to suddenly discover that instability in its own form. Of course, *Bleak House* is not the only novel to have made that discovery. *Middlemarch*, for one, makes it as well, and a good deal more explicitly and consciously—and my argument, indeed, has been that all novels make it at least unconsciously. But no other novel, I believe, embodies that discovery so deeply nor takes it so seriously as *Bleak House*. For all George Eliot's talk about "egoism" (and she is of course fully aware that it is in the novelist's own egoism that the instability of the novel chiefly lies), she handles her subject with such apparent mastery that we are left feeling entirely secure—in her grasp of the problem, at any rate. Her very wisdom, or aura of wisdom, somehow seems to defuse the problem, and Victorian doubt is dispelled by the comforting voice of the Victorian sage. As we have seen, no such positive resolution of the conflict is allowed us at the end of *Bleak House*: its crises are unending, and the pit of insecurity it has pointed to beneath the surface of life remains ready to open up again with the next falling round of its world's perpetual peripety.

That pit of insecurity puts me in mind again of the lesser image I have used to describe the history and theory of the novel: the fog. The definition of the novel I have proposed is not intended to bring order to the novel so much as to work its inherent disorder into sharper definition. It continues to be a foggy subject simply because the tension between the empirical and the fictional or the real and the ideal continues, without sign of abatement, to be a real problem. The double perspective implicit in dwelling upon "the romantic side of familiar things" remains open, and rather than producing, as George Eliot, say, might have wished, a nicely stereoscopic view of things, may, as often as not, and as it does in *Bleak House,* result in a dizzying and uncanny double vision. As long as novels maintain their capacity to amuse us with their play between the empirical and the fictional, they will retain the capacity deeply to unsettle us, for as long as reality is something that *can* be played with, it will remain, like all toys—no matter of how highly serious or educational a kind—something that can be broken.

NOTES

ONE: INTRODUCTORY

1. In a review of *Sketches by Boz*, *Spectator*, Feb. 20, 1836, p. 183. Quoted by John Butt and Kathleen Tillotson, *Dickens at Work* (London: Methuen, 1957), p. 37.

2. G. K. Chesterton, *The Victorian Age in Literature* (London: Oxford University Press, 1946), p. 77.

3. Johnson, p. 22 and Philip Collins, *Dickens: Bleak House* (London: Macmillan, 1971), p. 73.

4. But see A. E. Dyson, *"Bleak House:* Esther Better not Born?" in Dyson, ed., *Charles Dickens: Bleak House, a Casebook* (Nashville: Aurora, 1970), pp. 244–73. This essay is an important exception, although Dyson's discussion and mine overlap but slightly.

5. Rpt. in *MP*, I, 113–14.

6. Rpt. in *MP*, I, 64–65.

7. E. T. Cook and A. Wedderburn, eds., *The Works of John Ruskin* (London: George Allen, 1902–12), 37, 7.

8. Forster, VI, 4.

9. On Dickens and ghosts, see Harry Stone, "The Unknown Dickens: With a Sampling of Uncollected Writings," *Dickens Studies Annual*, vol. 1, ed. Robert B. Partlow, Jr. (Carbondale: Southern Illinois University Press, 1970), pp. 1–22, esp. pp. 8–12; on mesmeric clairvoyance, see Fred Kaplan, *Dickens and Mesmerism: The Hidden Springs of Fiction* (Princeton: Princeton University Press, 1975), *pp.* 152–53; on Spontaneous Combustion, see Trevor Blount, "Dickens and Mr. Krook's Spontaneous Combustion," *Dickens Studies Annual*, vol. 1, pp. 183–211 and Gordon S. Haight, "Dickens and Lewes on Spontaneous Combustion," *Nineteenth Century Fiction*, 10 (1955), 53–63.

10. Nonesuch Letters, 2, 203 (Feb. 1, 1850) and Forster, VII, 2 (Aug. 8, 1852).

TWO: SUSPENDED ANIMATION

1. J. Hillis Miller, "The Fiction of Realism: *Sketches by Boz, Oliver Twist,* and Cruikshank's Illustrations," in *Dickens Centennial Essays,* ed. Ada Nisbet and Blake Nevius (Berkeley: University of California Press, 1971), pp. 85–154, and Steven Marcus, "Language into Structure: Pickwick Revisited," *Daedalus,* 101 (1972), 183–202.

2. *Bleak House* (Harmondsworth: Penguin, 1971), p. 11.

3. *Ibid.,* p. 22.

4. *Ibid.*

5. *Ibid.,* p. 23.

6. Quoted by Robert Garis, *The Dickens Theatre: A Reassessment of the Novels* (Oxford: Clarendon, 1967), pp. 15–16. The quotation is from George Gissing, *Charles Dickens* (New York, 1924), p. 228.

7. Garis, p. 16.

8. The classic demonstration of the topicality not only of Chancery abuses, but also of all the major social satire in *BH* is in John Butt and Kathleen Tillotson, "The Topicality of *Bleak House,*" in *Dickens at Work* (London: Methuen, 1957), pp. 177–200. Their work follows the lead of Humphry House in *The Dickens World* (Oxford: Oxford University Press, 1942). Notable among the more recent scholars of *BH*'s topicality are Philip Collins, K. J. Fielding, and Trevor Blount. Their numerous essays can easily be located in the bibliographies listed in the bibliographical note at the end of this volume.

9. It is particularly instructive to compare the first few paragraphs of the novel with Milton's description of Chaos in Book II of *Paradise Lost.* See esp. ll. 890–900, 907–19, 927–42, 947–50. I use the edition by Merrit Y. Hughes (New York: Odyssey, 1962), which follows the second edition of 1674.

10. J. Hillis Miller in *Charles Dickens: The World of his Novels* (1958; rpt. Bloomington: Indiana University Press, 1969), pp. 187–90, is the first critic to discuss a pattern of circular repetitions in *BH.* H. M. Dalseki in *Dickens and the Art of Analogy* (New York: Schocken Books, 1970), pp. 156–90, has dis-

cussed the circles of *BH* at length in what I think is the best of recent essays on the novel.

11. Miller, *Charles Dickens*, p. 165.

12. There is also perhaps an allusion to the biblical Esther, also a queen, who "obtained favor in the sight of all them who looked upon her" (Esther 2:15.), for Esther Summerson seems to be explicitly recalling these words when she says that she "found some favour in [Allan Woodcourt's] eyes" (25).

13. This is what Freud refers to in *The Interpretation of Dreams* as secondary revision or elaboration, a function of both the dream-work and of waking life.

14. One of Esther's nicknames at Bleak House, of course, is "Little Old Woman" (8).

15. Miller, *Charles Dickens*, p. 164.

16. An analysis of the quite long description of Bleak House will show an incredible number of resonances not only with Chancery, but with all the worlds of the novel we have encountered thus far, as well as most of the other actual houses in the novel. In "The Titles for *Bleak House*," *The Dickensian*, 65 (1969), 84–89, George Ford has demonstrated many connections between Bleak House and the rest of the novel.

THREE: THE UNCANNY

1. Garrett Stewart's *Dickens and the Trials of the Imagination* (Cambridge, Mass.: Harvard University Press, 1974) is one of the most recent and best of such studies.

2. G. H. Lewes, "Dickens in Relation to Criticism," *Fortnightly Review*, 17 (Feb. 1872); rpt. in Stephen Wall, ed., *Charles Dickens: A Critical Anthology* (Harmondsworth: Penguin, 1970), pp. 191–202.

3. R. H. Hutton, "The genius of Dickens," *Spectator*, Feb. 7, 1874; rpt. in Wall, pp. 205–9.

4. Instantaneous appearances and disappearances are a regular feature of *BH*. Mr. Bucket's truly magical appearance (22) is the best example, perhaps, but there are many others. Lady Dedlock's sudden appearance in the keeper's lodge (18) and her equally sudden vanishing at the end of the tour of Nemo's

burying-ground (16) and the young man who "instantly evaporates" at a touch of Bucket's stick during his tour with Snagsby of Tom-all-Alone's (22) are only a few examples.

5. "The 'Uncanny,' " in *The Standard Edition of the Complete Psychological Works of Sigmund Freud*, ed. James Strachey (London: Hogarth, 1962–73), 17, 241. Subsequent references will simply be to The Standard Edition.

6. In the fifth of the *Introductory Lectures on Psycho-Analysis*, The Standard Edition, 15, 98.

7. The Standard Edition, 17, 245. The last pair of brackets are in the original.

8. *Ibid.*, p. 225.

9. *Ibid.*

10. The ghost of Tom Jarndyce haunts Chancery, Bleak House itself, and Tom-all-Alone's (which is named after him). Chesney Wold is haunted by the ghost of the Ghost's Walk, and even the most peripheral houses are haunted by a past that refuses to die or that its inhabitants refuse to let die. The Bayham Badgers' is haunted by Mrs. Badger's first two husbands, Captain Swosser and Professor Dingo, the Bagnets' and George's shooting gallery by the ghost of the military (Just as George himself is haunted by the ghost of his own military moustaches), and the Turveydrops' establishment is haunted by the ghost of the Prince Regent.

11. These of course are the words from which Carlyle famously and falsely derives "king" in *On Heroes, Hero-Worship, and the Heroic in History* (see Lectures I and VI).

12. The Standard Edition, 17, 245. The brackets are in the original.

13. This brief vignette anticipates not only Lady Dedlock's meeting with Esther in the same lodge, but another scene in the rain, the final reunion of mother, father, and child, when it will be the child who chases the mother, dead at the entrance to the place where Hawdon is buried, and then runs into the arms of her future husband, "wrapped in a cloak" (59).

14. The Standard Edition, 17, 249.

15. *Ibid.*, pp. 250–51.

16. "A Disturbance of Memory on the Acropolis," The Standard Edition, 22, 245.

17. *Ibid.*

18. *Jokes and their Relation to the Unconscious*, The Standard Edition, 7, 166. Original in italics.

19. Merton M. Gill and Margaret Brenman, *Hypnosis and Related States: Psychoanalytic Studies in Regression* (New York: John Wiley and Sons, 1966), pp. 115 and 157–67. I have made considerable use of Drs. Gill and Brenman's useful summaries of the psychoanalytic literature on hypnoid states.

20. Since this chapter was written, Fred Kaplan's *Dickens and Mesmerism: The Hidden Springs of Fiction* (Princeton: Princeton University Press, 1975) has appeared. It is the most thorough description and documentation of Dickens's interest in hypnosis we have had. I hope the use I have made of psychoanalysis will be seen as adding something to Kaplan's account as well as broadening the range of phenomena that can be linked with mesmerism. Dickens's intuitive understanding of hypnosis, I would argue, makes him a better psychologist than the professional mesmerists of his day.

21. The literature on Esther's psychology is quite large. Modern critical opinions about Esther were almost unanimously unfavorable until James Broderick and John Grant's "The Identity of Esther Summerson," *Modern Philology*, 55 (1958), 252–58. William Axton's "The Trouble with Esther," *Modern Language Quarterly*, 26 (1965), 545–57, struggles with the same issue. One of the most sensible of the defenses of Esther is Martha Rosso's "Dickens and Esther," *The Dickensian*, 65 (1969), 90–94.

22. Coutts Letters, p. 215. Johnson, by the way, is wrong in calculating, as he says in his note to this letter (of Nov. 19, 1852), that Dickens was referring to *BH* no. 9. The number for December, which Dickens was writing at this time, was in fact no. 10 (30–32). Johnson, on the basis of this miscalculation, assumes the "great turning idea" to have been the discovery of Esther's identity, which is made by the reader in no. 9.

23. One of the features of her little maid that Esther returns to again and again is the roundness of her staring eyes, recalling Esther's doll, as when she says in the same chapter, "If Charley could only have made the letters in her copy as round as the eyes with which she looked into my face, they would have been excellent." Charley's plaintive "O miss, it's my doing! It's my doing!" echoes Esther's childhood self-accusations: "What did I do to [my mother]? How did I lose her? Why am I so different from other children, and why is it my fault, dear godmother?" (3).

157

24. H. M. Daleski, *Dickens and the Art of Analogy* (New York: Schocken Books, 1970), p. 185.

25. Gill and Brenman, *Hypnosis and Related States*, p. 13.

26. A note for the psychoanalytically inclined. In "Dickens's Excremental Vision," *Victorian Studies*, 13 (1970), 339–54, Michael Steig has extensively discussed *BH* in psychoanalytic terms. His finding, anticipated by Humphry House's diagnosis in *The Dickens World* (Oxford: Oxford University Press, 1942), pp. 242–43, is that *BH* manifests the traits of an anal character. And there can be no question that Steig is right in seeing a profusion of anal imagery in the novel. I would argue, however, that there is a profusion not only of anal, but also of oral and phallic imagery as well. I see, in other words, an abundance of *pre-genital* imagery of all sorts, and this I believe strengthens the argument I have been making about Esther. Whereas Steig writes about Esther's "virtual sexlessness" (p. 354), I have argued that Esther's story is in fact about how, in spite of a horrendous childhood, she achieves sexuality, or, in psychoanalytic terminology, genitality. The *pre*-genital imagery in the novel represents to me, as it does in psychoanalytic theory, both the components out of which adult sexuality must be organized and the fixation points of neurotic development. But I want to stress that in any reading of the novel these are precisely what Dickens sees us as having to grow out of, and that he recognizes that growing out of them means a good deal more than simply having recourse to such reaction formations as the virtues, to use Steig's choice, of "purity and order" (p. 351). I might add that if we had to offer a diagnosis of Dickens, it would lie more toward hysteria than toward an anal—or any pre-genital—character type. This would be in line as well with my (and Kaplan's) arguments about the importance of hypnoid phenomena in the work and in the life.

27. Chapter 24, which gives us Esther's account of Chancery, is perhaps the best example of this. But in fact from very early on she has been viewing the novel's grotesques with characteristically Dickensian eyes—as, for example, when she says of Mr. Turveydrop that "I almost believe I saw creases come into the whites of his eyes" (14).

28. In *Dickens: The Dreamer's Stance* (Ithaca: Cornell University Press, 1965). Stoehr's analysis of the doubling of characters in *BH* is the best we have had, and in my account of the Esther–Mlle. Hortense–Lady Dedlock triad below I have made considerable use of his findings.

29. See especially Philip Collins, *Dickens and Crime* (Bloomington: Indiana University Press, 1962), pp. 290–319; Edmund Wilson, *The Wound and the Bow* (New York: Oxford University Press, 1965), pp. 68–85; and Forster, XI, 2. The passage in which Dickens elucidates double consciousness occurs in *Edwin Drood*, ch. 3.

FOUR: A BIOGRAPHICAL EXCURSION

1. Indeed, the life has had the sort of subsequent history usually reserved for more purely literary productions. Mark Spilka has shown in *Dickens and Kafka: A Mutual Interpretation* (Bloomington: Indiana University Press, 1963) how much of *The Metamorphosis* has its origin in Kafka's reading of *David Copperfield*. He also argues convincingly that Kafka had read Forster's *Life*, but he omits to mention a number of details in Kafka's story that seem to come from Kafka's reading of Forster. Gregor Samsa's sister, in particular, whose musical studies at the Conservatory are such a strain on the family's finances, apparently has her original in Dickens's sister Fanny, who flourished at the Royal Academy of Music at precisely the time John Dickens was imprisoned for debt and Charles was relegated to working at Warren's Blacking.

2. Butt and Tillotson, pp. 189–93.

3. B. B. Valentine, "The Original of Hortense and the Trial of Marcia [sic] Manning for Murder," *The Dickensian*, 19 (1923), 21–22.

4. Trevor Blount, "*Bleak House* and the Sloane Scandal of 1851 Again," *Dickens Studies*, 3 (1967), 63–67.

5. John Suddaby, "The Crossing Sweeper in *Bleak House*: Dickens and the Original of Jo," *The Dickensian*, 8 (1912), 246–50.

6. Forster, V, 7 and II, 7.

7. K. J. Fielding and A. W. Brice, "Dickens and the Tooting Disaster," *Victorian Studies*, 12 (1961), 227–44.

8. F. G. Kitton, in *Charles Dickens: His Life, Writings and Personality* (London: Caxton, n.d. [1902?]), p. 224, tells us that Dickens borrowed his friend John Forster's lodgings at 58 Lincoln's Inn Fields for Tulkinghorn's chambers. B. W. Matz, in *Dickensian Inns and Taverns* (New York: Scribner's 1922), pp. 169–71, identifies the Old Ship Tavern of Chichester Rents—itself the original of the street in which Krook has his shop—as the original of the Sol's

Arms. The editors of The Pilgrim Letters (1, 45 and n.) discuss Coavinses and its original, Sloman's sponging house, at 4, Cursitor Street. Different originals have been identified for Nemo's burying-ground by Walter Dexter in "Poor Jo's Churchyard Identified," *The Dickensian*, 25 (1929), 143, following a letter by Dickens (to Miss Palfrey, April 4, 1868), Nonesuch Letters, 3, 642, and W. L. Gadd in "The Topography of *Bleak House*," *The Dickensian*, 26 (1930), 207–12.

9. Robert Langton, *The Childhood and Youth of Charles Dickens* (Manchester: pvt. ptd., 1883), pp. 59–60.

10. Engels describes the street in *The Condition of the Working Class in England*, trans. W. O. Henderson and W. H. Chaloner (Stanford: Stanford University Press, 1968), p. 58.

11. Johnson, p. 47.

12. *Report by the Commissioners appointed to inquire into the practice of Chancery. Parliamentary Papers*, 1826, 15, Appendix A, p. 273.

13. Johnson takes his date for establishing when the first ideas of *BH* occurred to Dickens by following a letter to Miss Coutts on Aug. 22, 1851 (Johnson, p. 727 and Coutts Letters, p. 185). My date is taken from a letter to Mary Boyle, MDGH Letters (Feb. 21, 1851).

14. Johnson, p. 712.

15. Stone, pp. 36–43.

16. *HW*, April 23, 1853, and rpt. in *MP*. The best modern account of the Home is in Philip Collins, *Dickens and Crime* (Bloomington: Indiana University Press, 1968), pp. 94–116, and see also the Coutts Letters, *passim*.

17. Coutts Letters, p. 120.

18. *Ibid.*, p. 192, *et passim*. Especially moving is the case of Frederick Maynard, pp. 274–83, 290–92.

19. In this and the following I have followed the accounts of Forster, VI, 5, and Johnson, pp. 719–39.

20. Nonesuch Letters, 2, 391.

21. Forster, VI, 6, Johnson, p. 744, and Kitton, p. 201.

22. Johnson, p. 745 and MDGH Letters (to Frank Stone, July 20, 1851).

NOTES TO PAGES 102–12

23. MS in the collection of the Pierpont Morgan Library, New York (to Henry Austin, Sept. 19, 1851), quoted by Johnson, p. 748.

24. See Duane DeVries' edition of the novel for the most complete list of Dickens's discarded titles for *BH*, and George Ford, above, chapter 2, n. 16.

25. Johnson, p. 730.

26. *Mr. and Mrs. Charles Dickens: His Letters to Her*, ed. Walter Dexter (London: Constable, 1935), pp. 150–51.

27. *Ibid.*, p. 152.

28. Johnson, p. 731. It is because Dickens refers to his father's operation as "the most terrible . . . known in surgery" that I conjecture that his father's complaint was bladder stones. For the most feared operation in the nineteenth century, both because of its physical and emotional pain, was that performed to remove stones in the bladder, which were reached in men through an incision made between the anus and the scrotum.

29. So named by Lionel Stevenson in "Dickens's Dark Novels, 1851–1857," *Sewanee Review*, 50 (1943), 398–409.

30. Johnson, p. 732, and see also Dexter, *Mr. and Mrs.*, p. 153.

31. The first (*HW*, April 26, 1851) is rpt. in Stone, 1, 253–74 and the second (*HW*, June 14, 1851) is rpt. in *RP*. See also Nonesuch Letters 2, 318 and MDGH Letters (to Wills, April 3, 1851).

32. "Night Walks," *AYR* (July 21, 1860); rpt. in *The Uncommercial Traveller*. My connecting the night-walks at the time of Dickens's father's death with the essay in *The Uncommercial Traveller* is to some extent conjectural, and so far as I know no previous writer has made the connection. Several years intervene, of course, between John Dickens's death and the writing of the essay. But I am unable to find any other March in Dickens's life before the writing of the essay that fits the circumstances described in it so well.

33. *Macbeth*, II.ii.35–40 in the New Cambridge Edition.

34. *HW*, Oct. 30, 1852; rpt. in *RP*.

35. The "great actor and dear friend" was of course Macready, who had given his farewell performance—as Macbeth—in Feb. 1851.

36. In this connection, Forster supplies us with an interesting footnote: "Anything more completely opposed to the Micawber type [than Dickens's person-

161

ality] could hardly be conceived, and yet there were moments (really and truly only moments) when the fancy would arise that if the conditions of his life had been reversed, something of a vagabond existence (using the word in Goldsmith's meaning) might have supervened. It would have been an unspeakable misery to him, but it might have come nevertheless. The question of hereditary transmission had a curious attraction for him, and considerations connected with it were frequently present to his mind" (VIII, 2).

37. This double view of Chancery is felt by Murray Krieger to be a weakness of the novel. It seems to me on the contrary a strength—and indeed the point. See *The Tragic Vision* (New York: Holt, Rinehart and Winston, 1960), pp. 138–40.

38. Philippe Ariès, *Western Attitudes toward Death: From the Middle Ages to the Present*, trans. Patricia M. Ranum (Baltimore: Johns Hopkins University Press, 1974).

39. Nonesuch Letters, 2, 203 (Feb. 1, 1850).

40. Forster, VII, 2 (Aug. 8, 1852).

41. *Ibid.*, VI, 6, and Johnson, pp. 730–32.

42. MDGH Letters (April 19, 1851).

43. See the title and accompanying footnote to Book II, Section I of Chauncey Hare Townshend's *Facts in Mesmerism* (London, 1840): "Mesmeric Somnambulism, or, More Properly, Sleepwaking." The note reads: "Dr. Elliotson, in the chapter on mesmerism in his PHYSIOLOGY, has adopted the term *sleepwaking*, because walking is but one result of the combination of the waking with the sleeping state, and because in this state persons may not walk, or may even be unable to walk." Elliotson's *Human Physiology*, 5th Edition (London, 1840) was among Dickens's books at his death. See J. H. Stonehouse, ed., *Catalogue of the Library of Charles Dickens from Gadshill: Reprinted from Sotheran's 'Price Current of Literature' Nos. CLXXIV and CLXXV* (London: Piccadilly Fountain Press, 1935). Dickens was familiar too with Townshend's book and indeed a close friend of his. It was to Townshend that Dickens dedicated *Great Expectations*. And see above, chapter 3, n. 20.

44. "Lyons, the Rhone, and the Goblin of Avignon," *Pictures from Italy*.

45. "Avignon to Genoa," *Ibid.*

FIVE: THE NOVEL AND THE NOVEL

1. For informative accounts of the influence of Dickens's childhood reading in the terrific, see R. D. McMaster, "Dickens and the Horrific," *The Dalhousie Review*, 38 (1958), 18–28 and Harry Stone, "Dark Corners of the Mind: Dickens's Childhood Reading," *The Hornbook*, 39 (1963), 306–21.

2. See above, chapter 2, note 2.

3. William James, *The Varieties of Religious Experience*, Lectures 6 and 7.

4. Ian Watt, *The Rise of the Novel* (Berkeley: University of California Press, 1959), p. 32.

5. *Ibid.*

6. *Ibid.*, p. 33. I have omitted the footnotes.

7. *Tom Jones*, II, 1.

8. Clara Reeve, *The Progress of Romance*, rpt. in Miriam Allott, *Novelists on the Novel* (London: Routledge and Kegan Paul, 1965), p. 47.

9. Robert Scholes and Robert Kellogg, *The Nature of Narrative* (New York: Oxford University Press, 1968), p. 15.

10. W. M. Thackeray, *The Letters and Private Papers of William Makepeace Thackeray*, coll. and ed. Gordon N. Ray (Cambridge, Mass.: Harvard University Press, 1945–46), 2, 772–73.

11. "Romance," in *The Encyclopedia Britannica, Supplement* (1824), and rpt. in *Miscellaneous Prose Works*, ed. J. G. Lockhart (Edinburgh, 1834–36), 6.

12. Scott's discussion about the romantic and the familiar could be easily enlarged to describe the aims of all art. It would then parallel the self-conscious program of Wordsworth in the Preface to *Lyrical Ballads* (and as described by Coleridge in *Biographia Literaria*) which in turn anticipates interests of various Russian formalists—notably Victor Shlovsky, whose notion of defamiliarization is in many ways analogous to the definition of the novel I am working with here. Indeed, the greatest weakness of that definition is, no doubt, that it can easily be extended to other genres. But its concomitant strength then would be that it accounts for why the novel became the predominant form of the nineteenth century.

A BIBLIOGRAPHICAL NOTE

There are such good bibliographies of Dickens in general and *Bleak House* in particular already in print that it would be wasteful to duplicate them here. I have included all authors cited in the text in the Index rather than giving a separate list of works cited. The best general Dickens bibliography is Philip Collins's in *The New Cambridge Bibliography of English Literature*, Volume 3, ed. George Watson (Cambridge: Cambridge University Press, 1969), 779–850. The most complete *Bleak House* bibliography is in Duane DeVries' edition of the novel for The Crowell Critical Library (New York: T. Y. Crowell, 1971). An earlier, but excellent bibliographical essay is Ada Nisbet's "Charles Dickens" in *Victorian Fiction: A Guide to Research*, ed. Lionel Stevenson (Cambridge, Mass.: Harvard University Press, 1966). This is currently being updated (to 1975) by Philip Collins for a revised edition of the guide under the general editorship of George Ford. The most complete one-volume Dickens bibliography is Joseph Gold's *The Stature of Dickens: A Centenary Bibliography* (Toronto: University of Toronto Press, 1971), but the most exhaustive bibliographical information can be found by consulting *The Dickensian* and *Dickens Studies Newsletter*. Frank T. Dunn has compiled an extremely useful *Cumulative Analytical Index to the Dickensian, 1905–74* (Hassocks: Harvester Press, 1976).

I will not rehearse here the list of classic Dickens criticism, but readers with an interest in the history of Dickens criticism should certainly read George Ford's *Dickens and His Readers* (Princeton: Princeton University Press, 1955 and rpt. New York: Norton, 1965), which itself deserves a place on any list of Dickensian classics.

In addition to the essays and books by Daleski, Kaplan, Marcus,

BIBLIOGRAPHICAL NOTE

Miller, Steig, and Stewart cited in the text, a very large number of Dickens studies have of course appeared too recently to be included in the bibliographies mentioned above. Among the more important of these are Barbara Hardy's *The Moral Art of Dickens* (New York: Oxford University Press, 1970), F. R. and Q. D. Leavis's *Dickens the Novelist* (London: Chatto and Windus, 1970), and Alexander Welsh's *The City of Dickens* (Oxford: Clarendon, 1971). The centenary year of 1970 also saw a profusion of celebratory picture books. In the case of E. W. F. Tomlin, ed., *Charles Dickens 1812–1870: A Centennial Volume* (New York: Simon and Schuster 1969) and Angus Wilson, *The World of Charles Dickens* (New York: Viking, 1970), scholars will be as pleased with the text as with the illustrations. Three collections of essays for the centenary also deserve mention for their generally high quality: Ada Nisbet and Blake Nevius, eds., *Dickens Centennial Essays* (Berkeley: University of California Press, 1971); Robert B. Partlow, Jr., ed., *Dickens the Craftsman* (Carbondale: Southern Illinois University Press, 1970); and Michael Slater, ed., *Dickens 1970* (London: Chapman and Hall, 1970). 1970 also saw the first volume of the *Dickens Studies Annual* which is now back in business after something happily turned up. The January 1973 (Vol. 69, part 1) number of *The Dickensian* and the September 1975 (Vol. 6, no. 3) number of *Dickens Studies Newsletter* are each almost entirely *Bleak House* issues, and are representative of the most recent *Bleak House* criticism.

Finally, the psychoanalytically-inclined may want to consult *Hartford Studies in Literature*, vol. 8, no. 1 (1976), which is devoted to a 1975 MLA Seminar on psychoanalytic criticism of Dickens, and Charles Kligerman, "The Dream of Charles Dickens," *Journal of the American Psychoanalytic Association*, 18(1970), 783–99.

INDEX

Allan's Court (Manchester), 96
All the Year Round, 8, 107
Ariès, Philippe, 114, 162
Austen, Jane, 129
Austin, Henry, 102, 161
Avignon, 118, 122
Axton, William, 157

Badger, Bayham and Mrs. (*BH*), 55, 83, 156
Bagnet, Matthew (*BH*), 84, 156
Bagnet, Mrs. (*BH*), 88, 94, 156
Barbary, Miss (*BH*), 42-43, 75, 79, 87, 90; as inquisitor, 73; her celibacy, 83; her death, 34-37; as double of Lady Dedlock, 62, 89
Barnaby Rudge, 104, 118, 126-27
Beadnell, George and Maria, 101
Biographia Literaria, 163
Bleak House, 25, 45, 85, 103, 120-21, 155, 156. *See also* Houses
Bleak House. *See* Causal relations; Celibacy; Chance; Chaos; Charity; Children; Circularity; *Déjà vu*; Double narration; Doubles; Dreams; Duty; Faith; Fog; Ghosts; Gothic; Houselessness; Houses; Hypnoid states; Inquisitions; Magic; Megalosaurus; Mesmerism; Mirroring of images; Mourning; Parents; Peripety; Philanthropy; Punning; Reform; Suspended animation; Topicality; Tours; Uncanny; *also names of characters, locales*
Blount, Trevor, 153, 154, 159

Blower, Joseph, 96-97
Blowers, Mr. (*BH*), 96
Borrioboola-Gha (*BH*), 39, 60
Boyle, Mary, 160
Boythorn, Lawrence (*BH*), 83, 95, 121
Brenman, Margaret, 157-58
Brice, A. W., 159
Broderick, James, 157
Brontë, Emily, 129
Bucket, Inspector (*BH*), 12, 50, 55, 121-22; his childlessness, 83; hunts down Lady Dedlock, 69, 90; his hypnotic powers, 73-75; his magicality, 75, 88, 155-56; his original, 94, 107
Bulwer-Lytton, Edward (Baron Lytton), 100-101
Burdett-Coutts, Baroness. *See* Coutts
Burying-ground (*BH*). *See* Hawdon
Butt, John, 94, 153, 154, 159

Carlyle, Thomas, 3, 156
Carstone, Richard (*BH*), 17, 26, 37, 53-54, 76, 83
Carton, Sidney (*A Tale of Two Cities*), 87
Castle of Otranto, The, 144-45
Catholicism, 123
Causal relations, 40-44, 60, 62-63, 71, 91, 122
Celibacy, 83
Chadband, Rev. (*BH*), 4
Chance, 20, 29, 35
Chancellor, the Lord (*BH*), 22, 26-27, 30, 36-37, 45, 69, 73
Chancery Commission of 1826, 96-97, 160

167

INDEX

Chancery, Court of, 16-17, 54, 59-60, 79, 89, 154, 156; as seen by Esther, 158; and hypnoid states, 72; and inquisitions, 121-22; in opening no., 20-23, 26-28, 30, 34; and reform, 94; its topicality vs. symbolism, 113-14, 162

Chaos, 20, 39, 44, 113-14, 154

Charity, 59-60, 115-16

Charley (*BH*). *See* Neckett

Chatham, 95

Chesney Wold (*BH*), 23, 25, 30, 41, 52-53, 61-63, 77, 81, 120-21, 156; its keeper's lodge, 63-64, 73, 76, 156. *See also* Ghost's Walk; Rockingham Castle

Chester, Edward (*Barnaby Rudge*), 105

Chesterton, G. K., 1, 6, 153

Children, 83-84

Child's History of England, A, 101

Cholera, 96

Christmas Books, 8

Circularity, 20-28, 32, 33-34, 37, 40, 44-45, 60, 85-86, 87, 112, 154-55

Clare, Ada (*BH*), 26, 37, 53, 63, 76, 83

Clenham house (*Little Dorrit*), 104

Coavinses (*BH*) 95, 160

Coleridge, Samuel Taylor, 163

Collins, Philip, 1, 153, 154, 159, 160, 165

Copperfield, David, 88, 93

Coutts, Angela Burdett, 76, 98-100, 102, 160

Daleski, H. M., 154-55, 158

Darnay, Charles (*A Tale of Two Cities*), 87

Darwin, Charles, 19

David Copperfield, 98, 100, 159

Debilitated cousin, the (*BH*), 73

Dedlock cousins, the (*BH*), 121

Dedlock, Lady Honoria (*BH*), 30, 41, 69, 83, 92, 94-95, 155; and causal relations, 39, 42; and circularity, 26, 30; as double of Miss Barbary, 42-43, 62, 89; as

Esther's mother, 36, 43-44, 61-64, 76, 78, 81, 89; first view of, 26-27, 31, 64, 156; her "freezing mood," 24, 36-37, 90; her recognition of Hawdon's handwriting, 29, 35; and houselessness, 105; hunting down, 38, 69, 90; and the murder, 73, 89-90, 112; her resemblance to Esther and Mlle. Hortense, 50-53, 56, 71, 89-91, 123; her tour of Hawdon's lodgings, 55, 121

Dedlock, Lady Morbury (*BH*), 25

Dedlock, Sir Leicester (*BH*), 25, 29, 83, 121

Dedlock, Volumnia (*BH*), 83

Defoe, Daniel, 129, 132-34, 135-37, 139

Déjà vu, 45, 50-56, 61, 63, 67, 76

Depersonalization, 67, 78

Derealization, 67

Devonshire, William, Duke of, 101

Devonshire Terrace (London), 102

DeVries, Duane, 161, 165

Dexter, Walter, 160, 161

Dickens, Catherine (Mrs. Charles Dickens), 105-6

Dickens, Charles: biographical events surrounding his writing of *BH*, 93-123 (amateur theatricals, 100-103; family illnesses and deaths, 105-7, 111-13, 116-17, 118, 161; first ideas of *BH*, 98; house-hunting, 102-3; insomnia, 107-11; interest in mesmerism, 117-18, 153, 162; periodical writing, 98; philanthropic activity, 98-100; visit to Avignon, 118-23); quality of his imagination, 47-50; psychoanalytic considerations about, 49, 111-13, 117-18, 158; relation between life and work, 93-94; his use of sources, 94-97. *See also* names of writings, characters, family, acquaintances, places

Dickens, Dora Annie, 116-17

Dickens, Fanny, 159

168

INDEX

Dickens, John: his imprisonment, 93, 159; his illness and death, 105-7, 111-13, 116, 118, 161

Dingo, Professor (*BH*), 156

Distortion, psychic, 67-68

Dolly (*BH*), 30, 69, 73, 79, 157

Dostoevsky, Fyodor, 49

Double narration, 14-15, 38, 54-55, 87

Doubles, 50-51, 85, 87-92

Dreams, 9, 49, 50, 57, 69, 75, 81, 109-10, 115, 117, 120, 155

Dunn, Frank T., 165

Duty, 60

Dyson, A. E., 153

Ego, splittings of, 76-84. *See also* Doubles

Eliot, George. *See* Mary Ann Evans

Elliotson, John, 117, 162

Epic, 141-42

Evans, Mary Ann (pseud. George Eliot), 129, 130, 150

Every Man in his Humour, 100

Examiner, The, 3

Exeter Hall, 94

Faith, 113, 115-16

Family romance, the, 86

Field, Inspector, 107

Fielding, Henry, 14, 129, 135-36, 139, 143, 145

Fielding, K. J., 154, 159

Flaubert, Gustave, 131

Flite, Miss (*BH*), 22, 39, 120; on Chancery, 17, 23, 72; and *déjà vu*, 53, 55-56; parallels with other characters, 36, 83, 90

Fog, 16, 21-22, 27, 31, 34

Ford, George H., 155, 161, 165

Forster, John, 153, 154, 159, 162; on Dickens's attitude toward father, 161-62; as Dickens's confidant, 9, 115; his lodgings, 159

Fortune, 20. *See also* Chance

Fortunes of Nigel, The, 146

French Revolution, 141-42

Freud, Sigmund, 19; on dreams, 49, 155; on jokes, 68, 157; on the uncanny, 56-58, 61, 63, 65-67, 86, 156

Gadd, W. L., 160

Garis, Robert, 13, 16, 154

Genre, change in notion of, 140-41

George IV, 156

George, Mr. (*BH*). *See* Rouncewell, George

Ghosts, 8, 156

Ghost's Walk, the (*BH*), 25, 82, 156

Gill, Merton M., 157, 158

Gissing, George, 16, 154

Goblin of Avignon (*Pictures from Italy*), 118-24, 162

Gold, Joseph, 165

Gordon Riots, 104

Gothic, the, 118, 126, 144

Gotschalk, Emmely, 115

Grant, James, 157

Great Expectations, 129, 162

Gridley, Mr. (*BH*), 17, 36, 55, 83, 90, 121

Guild of Literature and Art, 100-101, 103

Guppy, Mr. (*BH*), 52, 71-72, 76. *See also* Stevens

Guster (*BH*), 72-73, 83, 95

Haight, Gordon S., 153

Hardy, Barbara, 166

Hawdon, Capt. (*BH*), 29, 35, 55, 83, 105, 121; his burying-ground, 79-80, 90, 95, 121, 160

Hawthorne, Nathaniel, 138

Heep, Uriah (*David Copperfield*), 88

Hogarth, Mary, 123

Hogg, James, 126

Home for Homeless Women. *See* Urania Cottage

INDEX

INDEX

171

INDEX

INDEX